GHOSTS AND LEGENDS OF HOLLYWOOD

BRIAN CLUNE

Published by Haunted America
A Division of The History Press
Charleston, SC
www.historypress.com

The Exorcist. Terri Clune.
Front cover: The Pantages Theatre, located at Hollywood and Vine, Hollywood, California. *The Jon B. Lovelace Collection of California Photographs in Carol M. Highsmith's America Project, Library of Congress, Prints and Photographs Division*.
Back cover: The Hollywood sign is a landmark and American cultural icon located in Los Angeles, California. *The Jon B. Lovelace Collection of California Photographs in Carol M. Highsmith's America Project, Library of Congress, Prints and Photographs Division*.

Unless otherwise noted, all photos by Terri Clune.

First published 2023

Manufactured in the United States

ISBN 9781467155182

Library of Congress Control Number: 2023938395

The Hollywood sign is one of the most well-known signs in the world.

This book is dedicated to my wife, Terri. She has stuck with me through a lot and has supported me even when that support meant long periods away from each other. She has never wavered—although she admitted to it wobbling a little—in her love for me. Thank you for everything you do.

I also dedicate this book to all of the folks who work behind the scenes in the production of the movies that give us so much entertainment, laughter, drama and spine-tingling horror. Without all of these nameless grips, designers, makeup artists, costumers and so many more, we would not have these films to enjoy.

Monsters are real, ghosts are real too.
They live inside us, and sometimes they win.
—*Stephen King,* The Shining

CONTENTS

Acknowledgements   11
Introduction: California Dreamin'   13

PART I: CURSED HOLLYWOOD
1. Curse of the Best Actress Award   17
2. The Curse of *The Exorcist*   22
3. The Curse of *The Crow*   29
4. The Most Cursed Film in Hollywood   35

PART II: PROPHECIES AND PREMONITIONS
5. James Dean: A Race to the Death   45
6. Oliver Reed: A Drink to Die For   53
7. Sharon Tate, Jay Sebring, Premonitions and Murder   56
8. Carrie Fisher and the Force   63
9. John Lennon and the Number 9   67
10. Prince, Tupac and Naya Rivera   74

PART III: GHOSTS AND LEGENDS
11. Rudolph Valentino and Falcon Lair   83
12. The Strange Death and Curse of the Hot Toddy   93
13. The Mystery of the Houdini Estate   103
14. The Medieval Torture Museum   112
15. El Coyote Café   121

Contents

16. The Sad Spirit of Ramon Novarro   129
17. The Escape Hotel   136
18. The Mansion   146

Epilogue   151
Bibliography   153
About the Author   157

ACKNOWLEDGEMENTS

Even though Hollywood is very close to me, writing this book was harder than I figured it would be. But I had plenty of help along the way, which made it easier. First and, as always, I have to thank my acquisitions editor, Laurie Krill, for again putting up with my incessant babble and numerous inane questions. I still have no idea how she does it. My wife, on the other hand, has to put up with me; I have a paper that says so. Be that as it may, I could never do this without her support, companionship and counsel. She is also a great spellchecker when I forget that I have Siri and a word processer. Terri is also a great photographer and an even better first-round editor, helpful skills during the pre-publication process. Two gentlemen whom I must thank for their time, knowledge, tour guide ability and kindness are Robert Sanchez, general manager of the Medieval Torture Museum; and Lee Hill-Chan, general manager of the Escape Hotel. Thank you, guys, for giving me great info and insight and for allowing me to put your establishments in the book. Last but not least, I want to thank my readers. Without you, I couldn't keep writing, nor would I want to. You are what keeps me going and what keeps my mind occupied with what you might want to read next. From the bottom of my heart, thank you!

INTRODUCTION

CALIFORNIA DREAMIN'

Many people dream about coming to California. Some dream about seeing the Redwoods and rivers, the majestic mountains and the wild and rocky shorelines of Northern California. Others look to Southern California and its iconic beaches, classic Mexican architecture and wonderful south-of-the-border cuisine. But many folks come to California for one thing: Hollywood.

Tinseltown is more than an idea; it's a dream. Folks come to see their screen idols and the glitz and glamour of the red carpet. Some seek out famous locations such as Grauman's Chinese Theatre, with its hand- and footprints from Hollywood's past. People visit the studios, some now turned into amusement parks, and even the graveyards of the stars, many of which are haunted, like Hollywood Forever and Westwood Memorial Park. And many come to pursue their own dream, that of becoming the next big star and Hollywood millionaire. This dream, like so many others in which Hollywood is involved, often becomes a nightmare—one from which the dreamer can't wake.

There are many famous cities around the world. Indeed, America has more than a few of its own. But none of them comes close to the sheer horror that Hollywood—the sunny, glitzy and star-studded town in Southern California—can and has generated. Maybe this is a result of the competition inherent in the movie industry, especially in winning a role in a movie. From a minor part to the main role in the biggest blockbuster, the clash remains the same: cutthroat. This vying to get ahead is ever present in Tinseltown.

Could this be why Hollywood breeds so many curses? Dark legends abound in Hollywood about actors and actresses and cursed movies. The destruction caused by these curses can be annoying at the least, absolute at the worst and, on occasion, everlasting.

Other horrors occur in Hollywood, where murders are plentiful, as are the ghosts of the victims. The spirits of movie stars long dead also appear. From the movie studios where the famous plied their trade, to the restaurants where they shared their last meals and the homes where they loved, lived and died, Hollywood's past elite remain to scare the unsuspecting who tread on their sacred grounds. Even the Hollywood sign, that icon that welcomes tourists and hopefuls to the land of dreams, has its own ghost who forever wanders in despair for lost roles and forgotten dreams.

Then there are the legends that revolve around movie stars who seem to have had the precognitive ability to predict their death or who have had spirits warn them of their impending demise. Fans of these actors and musicians marvel as tales are told of their idol's accuracy in predicting the day and time of their death. Some fans elevate their idols to the status of mystical beings. Other legends, like that of Sharon Tate and Jay Sebring, tell how a dead Hollywood insider might have come back to give a dire warning in the hopes of sparing someone from suffering the same fate that took his own life. These are legends, but they are compelling in their telling.

Hollywood is the land of dreams and make-believe but also home to nightmares and horrors both real and created. Death, murder, turmoil and suicide lie hidden behind the silver screen and beneath the red carpet. Pain and sorrow hide behind the posh mansions and wealthy estates, and murder and mayhem wait for the unsuspecting. Hollywood has it all. Keep reading if you dare. You'll learn about the sordid details and hidden specters that wait in the shadows of Tinseltown.

Part I

Cursed Hollywood

The dictionary defines the word *curse* as "a solemn utterance intended to invoke a supernatural power to inflict harm or punishment on someone or something." Although a somewhat technical summation, this definition gets to the heart of the matter: Curses are bad. Many folks don't believe in the magical aspect of a curse—me, for one. I believe that curses, once known, are self-fulfilling. If you think something will happen, you will make it happen. Others, however, believe so strongly in magic that, once cursed, they will do everything in their power to stop it. They will pay any price, commit any act—even murder—to be released from the curse. And this, of course, usually causes the curse to come to fruition.

Curses are bad enough. But combine a good old-fashioned curse with the over-amped egos and superstitions in Hollywood, and you have a mythos rivaled by none. Hollywood has always had its cast of colorful characters, both on and off the screen. And with these characters comes a whole host of beliefs, ranging from established religion to witchcraft, Druidism and voodooism. You name it, Hollywood has it. Mix in one of Hollywood's favorite protagonist groups, gypsies, and you have a veritable stew of bad omens, premonitions and, yes, curses. But what happens when a seeming curse hits Hollywood's grandest event, the Academy Awards? You get a curse that befalls only actresses, never actors. Could it be that Oscar is the ultimate misogynist? Or is it just a matter of bad luck?

The Biltmore Hotel, in downtown Los Angeles, was an early venue for the Academy Awards and where "Oscar" himself was born.

1

CURSE OF THE
BEST ACTRESS AWARD

The Oscar ceremony is by far the most anticipated night for those who work in Hollywood and for the fans of Tinseltown in general. More than the Golden Globes, the Academy Awards, where actors and actresses dress in $100,000 designer suits and gowns that would make King Solomon jealous, is a night when expectations of glory run high and huge movie contracts run through the minds of the nominees. And we can't forget to mention those after-parties. But if you are one of Hollywood's elite or up-and-coming actresses hoping for that coveted Best Actress Award, you might want to rethink accepting it if you are so honored by the Academy of Motion Picture Arts and Sciences. That is, if you love your partner and your career.

There is some dispute about the origins of the "Best Actress Curse." Some say that it began in 1929, when Mary Pickford, the second winner of the award, won for the film *Coquette*. At the time, Pickford was the biggest star in the world and seemed to be on every studio's A list. *Coquette* was Pickford's first "talkie." Many actors and actresses couldn't make the transition from the "silent" era into the new format, but Pickford's voice carried over well. But being the most sought-after star in Hollywood and having a huge fan base is nothing compared to a burgeoning curse. Just four years after winning the coveted award, Mary Pickford retired at the height of her career.

Some people claim that the curse began in the mid-1930s, after Luise Rainer won back-to-back Best Actress Awards. The first came for the 1936 MGM film *The Great Ziegfeld*. Many believe that since her role was

Luxury was always a part of the Academy Awards. Here, the interior of the Biltmore Hotel gives us just a glimpse.

a supporting role to that of actress Myrna Loy she should have not been nominated for Best Actress, but instead for Best Supporting Actress. After Rainer won over established stars such as Carole Lombard, Irene Dunne and Norma Shearer, many believed the voting had been rigged in Rainer's favor. After winning her second Best Actress Award, in 1937 for her portrayal of a Chinese woman in *The Good Earth*, this time over Barbara Stanwyck, Greta Garbo, Janet Gaynor and, again, Irene Dunne, an urban legend grew that many of the Hollywood actresses got together and cursed Luise Rainer. Whatever the status of this urban legend, the curse worked. Rainer was finished in Hollywood less than a year after being the only person up to that time to not only win two Academy Awards but also to win them back to back. Rainer did go on to appear on the stage and in films, even appearing on television, but her star power and her Hollywood fame were gone forever. The bad thing about curses is that they can't be controlled, and this one seems to have continued and has affected a majority of the actresses who followed.

Hattie McDaniel, best known for her portrayal as Mammy in the classic film *Gone with the Wind*, won the Best Supporting Actress Award for her role. After that, however, no one could separate her from the character, and the only roles she was offered were of maids—seventy-four, to be exact. The studios' typecasting never allowed for roles that could fully display her acting prowess to audiences. The award seemingly destroyed her ability to showcase her talent.

Another up-and-coming Black actress, and the first to win in the Best Actress category, Halle Berry, seemed to have broken a Hollywood glass ceiling of the Academy. But she found that after winning for her stunning portrayal in the movie *Monster's Ball*, roles, although they did not dry up, were a far cry from those the Academy considered worthy of awards. *Catwoman*, *Gothika* and *X-Men*, all popular films, were not the type to reach a broad spectrum of audience and were therefore limited in scope in terms of awards. Berry still has not reached the heights to which she once soared.

Catherine Zeta-Jones was one of the most-sought after actresses in Hollywood until she won for her role in the musical *Chicago*, after which parts all but vanished. Other actresses have seen their careers experience unexpected downward trajectories after winning at the Academy Awards, including Julia Roberts (*Erin Brockovich*), Natalie Portman (*Black Swan*), Nicole Kidman (*The Hours*), Charlize Theron (*Monster*) and even Helen Mirren (*The Queen*). Marcia Gay Harden said it best after winning for her role in the movie *Pollock* in 2001. "The Oscar is disastrous on a professional

Grauman's Chinese Theatre, with its cement imprints of famous celebrities' hands and feet spread out on its patio, was an obvious choice to host the Academy Awards in the past.

level. Suddenly the parts you're offered become smaller and the money less. There's no logic to it."

As bad as this curse may be for an actress's career, there is another aspect that is much worse. The curse seems to have a profound impact on the love life of the starlet who is unfortunate enough to win an Oscar. Actresses like Reese Witherspoon have had to deal with both of these unsavory results of winning on the big night.

There have been 266 married women who have won the Best Actress or Best Supporting Actress Award. Of those, 159 have had their relationships end shortly after winning. Some, like Witherspoon, have not only had their marriages end but have also seen their careers take a nosedive. Witherspoon won the award in 2006 for her portrayal of June Carter Cash in *Walk the Line*. Not only did her career almost immediately decline with roles in movies that flopped, such as *Four Christmases*, and being upstaged by an elephant in *Water for Elephants*, but also her marriage to fellow actor Ryan Phillippe fell apart eight months after winning. It seems that Ryan didn't mind giving extra attention to his female costars. After less than eight years of marriage, their union was over after Oscar came on the scene. Witherspoon was not the first recipient to have her relationship end with the awards and certainly wasn't the last.

Joan Crawford is widely believed to be the first actress struck by this second aspect of the curse, or what has come to be called the "Oscar love jinx." Shortly after winning the Best Actress Award for her role in the film *Mildred Pierce*, Crawford and her third husband, Phillip Terry, divorced in a very public affair in 1946. From this point, it appears, the floodgates opened for relationship destruction for many female Oscar winners. Halle Berry split from her second husband, singer Eric Benét, after which he entered rehab for sex addiction. Brie Larson, after winning in 2016, ended her relationship with fiancé Alex Greenwald. Hilary Swank, Susan Sarandon and Kate Winslet have all had their marriages end after winning on Oscar night. It appears that Sandra Bullock takes home the award for fastest breakup in Academy Award curse history. It took just ten days for Bullock to end her marriage with husband Jesse James after taking home the statuette. It seems that James had been having numerous affairs, but Bullock found out about them only after winning Best Actress.

Many will chalk these up to mere happenstance, but the sheer number of coincidences involved with the Oscars curse of the Best Actress is hard to ignore. As one who is leery about curses in the first place, even I have to wonder if there is something going on with the awards ceremony that

The Dolby Theater on Hollywood Boulevard has hosted the Academy Awards in years past and hosted it again in 2023.

actresses are better off avoiding. Of course, even with the supposed curse, it is still a great feeling to be honored by one's peers in the Academy and to be recognized for one's talent. It is up to my readers to decide if the curse gets the award for Best Home-Wrecker.

2
THE CURSE OF *THE EXORCIST*

The Academy Awards is not the only place where curses can be found in and around Hollywood. For as long as movies have been made, folks have talked about films that might be cursed. In the early days, tales of plagued movies came mostly from groups who thought moving pictures were, in and of themselves, the work of the devil. Fanatical Christians, country Baptist ministers and other religious people came out publicly against them, but no one really took them seriously. As the industry grew, more stories came out about films experiencing strange accidents, unexplained injuries to cast and crew, fires and other odd goings-on in the lives of the actors and actresses and on the set. Today, it is almost a given that some Hollywood films have been either cursed or touched by the hand of evil to the point that many people do not doubt that there is something paranormal at work in the studios of Tinseltown. There is one film that many believe was cursed by none other than the old Mesopotamian demon Pazuzu. I am, of course, speaking about *The Exorcist*.

By now, most people know that William Peter Blatty based the book *The Exorcist* on true events, but many still don't know the details regarding the actual exorcism that took place in St. Louis or that Father William Bowdern experienced lasting effects from the ritual. To protect those involved in the real case, Blatty changed their names as well as the location of the events. He also tried to keep the real family as far from the book and movie as possible. Blatty also changed the gender of the possessed child. Naturally, as time went by, and with the advent of the internet, his efforts have become moot. But he did try.

Blatty had gotten wind of the exorcism and conducted several interviews with those in the know. He also studied up on the Catholic ritual, the supposed demonic entity and the mythos from which the demon sprang. Several of the things Blatty included in his book occurred in the actual case, such as the strange voices coming out of the possessed, speaking in languages the child didn't know, as well as the words *help me* that appear on the character's stomach from within. All of these are said to have actually happened. (Bowdern's diary claims that words appeared many times a day during the actual exorcism.) Blatty also used the Ouija board in the film, which was said to have been used by the grandmother of the possessed boy. But this was later found to be untrue.

Blatty seems to have done his research, and the book he penned became a bestseller and a classic. The resulting movie became an instant success but drew the ire of religious groups around the world. The film was banned in every Middle Eastern country except Lebanon. Israel allowed the film but only in select theaters, and the Catholic Church condemned it as "evil." None of this stopped audiences from flocking to theaters to see this one-of-a-kind horror film. Mired in controversy and religious furor, it didn't take long for the film to gain a reputation for being associated with odd events happening to audience members. After tales were leaked from some of the crew who had worked on the film, stories of a curse spread at a rapid pace. It wasn't long before many people believed that one of the religious groups opposed to the book and the film had decided to punish Blatty and everyone involved with the evil events depicted. With everything that took place before and after the movie was released, it seems the curse might actually be true.

The Exorcist was filmed over a nine-month period. Although the real events took place in St. Louis, Blatty used Georgetown as the location in the book and script. Warner Bros. found the perfect house for the film, but as it could not accommodate the large cameras and other things required for moviemaking, a replica of the home's interior was built on a local soundstage. The first hint that something was not quite right with the movie's production came at about 2:30 a.m. on a Sunday when a pigeon, having somehow gotten into the soundstage, flew into a circuit box. The bird was electrocuted, which caused the circuit to arc and a fire to break out. The fire spread to all areas of the set and burned it to the ground. All areas, that is, except the bedroom of the character Regan, where the exorcism was to take place and where the demon would be "seen" the most. The bedroom was untouched by the blaze. The fire delayed filming by six weeks while the set was rebuilt. When the interior home set was finished, filming began again, but for only a few days. During a routine fire inspection of the new sprinkler system, it was found that it had broken down. Filming was set back an additional two weeks.

Many of the actors and crew involved with the film had troubles of their own while on the set. One of the carpenters working on rebuilding the set after the fire was cutting a board with a power saw and became distracted. He failed to see where his hand was in relation to the blade. He found out just how close when the spinning blade severed his thumb from his hand. Then, a lighting technician working on some overhead fixtures tried to dodge out of the way as one fixture began to fall; he was only partially successful. The fixture fell on the electrician's foot, cutting off one of his toes. It wasn't only the Georgetown set that had strange issues. The opening scenes of the movie take place in the Iraqi desert and were filmed on location. The original plan was to film during early and middle spring, when temperatures in that part of the world were still relatively mild. But there were delays in paperwork and with inspections of the equipment demanded by the Iraqi government. In addition, the bronze statue of the neo-Assyrian winged demon Pazuzu got lost in transit from Los Angeles and was shipped to Hong Kong instead of Baghdad. Filming in Iraq didn't begin until July. The statue has since become synonymous with the movie.

July is arguably the hottest part of the summer in the Middle Eastern desert, and temperatures began to reach 130° Fahrenheit, which took their toll on those not used to the heat. Of the eighteen crewmen who went to Iraq, William Friedkin, the film's director, lost half at one time or another due to dysentery, severe dehydration, cramps and even heatstroke. At one point, it seemed as if filming in the desert might have to be abandoned and moved to a set somewhere less arid. The delays put the movie in jeopardy and well over budget. It wasn't only the crew who had troubles while on the set. The cast also had its share of misfortunes during filming. Events that took place range from amusing to tragic, and some were downright deadly.

Ellen Burstyn, who played the possessed girl's mother, Chris MacNeil, sustained a permanent back injury during the stunt in which her daughter, Regan, played by actress Linda Blair, throws her across the room while a large dresser slides toward her in a menacing fashion. The shot made its way into the movie, and the look of pain on Burstyn's face is real. She was laid up in bed for several weeks, once again delaying production. Blair, only eleven years old, herself sustained long-term back injuries when a harness used to toss her around on the bed broke. A rumor arose that she suffered a nervous breakdown during filming, which, given her age at the time, is unusual. But the movie's subject matter may have contributed to her emotional problems. One of the more amusing accidents happened to Jason Miller, who played Father Damien Karras, the priest who has a crisis of faith before confronting the demon alongside Father Lankester Merrin. During the scene in which Regan/Pazuzu projectile-vomits onto Father Karras, the pea soup—yes, that is what was used—is supposed to splash onto his chest. But the tube used for the soup was misaligned and hit Miller in the face. The soup exploded into his eyes, mouth and nose, surprising everyone on set. Friedkin, seeing the pure look of shock and disgust on Miller's face and the way he hurriedly tried to clear the offending substance away, decided to keep the shot. To this day, his decision has caused countless audience members to lose their lunch. Other events related to the production are downright scary to contemplate and contribute to the theory of a curse.

There were several deaths associated with the film. Some can certainly be seen as coincidental. Linda Blair's grandfather died shortly after filming began, and Jason Miller's young son, actor Jason Patrick, was struck by a motorcycle while walking along a beach and was almost killed. The strange thing about this is that the motorcycle came out of nowhere, and the boy said he never saw or heard the bike before it hit him. An assistant cameraman who had been looking forward to the birth of his first child and who talked almost nonstop about it found out that the child was stillborn.

Because Friedkin wanted to make sure the audience could see the breath coming from the actors as they performed the exorcism scene, he had the room refrigerated while the cameras rolled. The refrigeration technician died shortly after these scenes were filmed. The custodian who took care of the set and the building was shot and killed in a botched holdup. Jack MacGowran played Burke Dennings, the fictional director of the film Chris MacNeil was starring in and who is murdered by the possessed Regan MacNeil when his head is twisted backward and he is thrown out the window of the house. McGowran died from influenza, and then, not even a month later, Vasiliki Maliaros, who played Father Karras's mother, died from "natural causes." Neither of these actors lived to see the movie's premiere. Things got so bad with the cast and crew starting to talk about evil on the set that Friedkin took drastic steps and brought in a priest to bless the soundstage and everyone involved with the movie. According to Ellen Burstyn, the blessing seemed to do the trick, and things went well afterward. The curse took its toll on the cast and crew of the movie during filming, but once *The Exorcist* was set for release, the curse came back in full force.

When *The Exorcist* was nominated for Best Picture, it sent waves of fear through religious institutions. It made Academy Awards history, as did the Roosevelt Hotel when the awards were held there.

During postproduction, strange things began to appear on the film. Odd double-exposure images began to appear superimposed over Linda Blair's images and odd voices sounded where no voices should have been. One crewman said, "There were strange images and visions that showed up on film that were never planned." Even the movie's director, Friedkin, claimed, "There are double exposures in the little girl's face at the end of one reel that are unbelievable." He never went on record to give details about this footage or say more beyond this statement.

After *The Exorcist* premiered, some in the cast were not done with experiencing strange goings-on. A few years after the film premiered, homosexuals began to be terrorized by a series of murders in and around New York City. The police were coming up short on suspects until an unrelated murder case offered evidence of the "bag murders." On September 14, 1977, film critic Addison Verrill was found stabbed and beaten to death in his New York apartment. The murderer was a thirty-eight-year-old x-ray technician, Paul Bateson. It turns out that Bateson played the x-ray tech who hooks up Linda Blair's character, Regan. He had been having thoughts of murder since appearing in the movie. He told investigators that he had no motive for the crimes; he felt like doing it for fun.

Mercedes McCambridge, the actress who voiced the demon Pazuzu, had her own tragic run-in with the curse. Her son John, a successful trader, was found to be embezzling funds from the trading company he worked for and placing them in his mother's account. John, knowing that he would be found guilty in a court of law, decided that prison was not for him and, in a moment of desperation, killed his wife and two young daughters before ending his own life. This happened more than ten years after the film's release, but when one considers that curses have no time limits, one has to wonder.

As bad as the curse was for the cast and crew of *The Exorcist*, it seems that it wasn't content to simply mess with the filmmakers. Many audiences have, over time, wondered if the curse has come to them. Many folks know that at the time the film was released it was unlike any movie—horror or otherwise—that anyone had ever seen. As such, many theaters kept barf bags on hand, as moviegoers would throw up during some scenes. Smelling salts were also kept handy, because folks were passing out in terror. So many people left theaters early that movie houses began to fear lawsuits. One suit was filed, but it was against Warner Bros. A moviegoer had passed out and broke her jaw; "the subliminal messages caused her injury," or so she claimed. The studio settled out of court. As bad as all of this was, worse things occurred during showings of the film.

An interesting thing happened in Rome, Italy. The first time *The Exorcist* was shown near the Vatican was at a theater that just happened to be between two churches. Although the day called for sunny weather, just before the theater opened, a sudden torrential rain came down, causing the area to be blanketed in an eerie and haunting lightning storm. At one point, a bolt of lightning struck one of the churches, causing a four-hundred-year-old crucifix to fall in the middle of the piazza, barely missing the large crowd of moviegoers.

Shortly after the full release of the film in the United Sates, reports of odd things happening to moviegoers grew at an alarming rate. One woman claimed that watching the film caused her body to miscarry. A psychologist reported a growing number of new patients who began having horrifying dreams of possession and experiencing demons talking to them in their sleep. A rumor began that just by watching the film one could become possessed by the devil. Numerous ushers had to be placed under doctor's care after working in theaters showing the movie, while others simply quit their jobs, never to return to the theater. Hallucinations, manic behavior and random acts of violence were all reported and attributed to watching the film.

No movie before or since has had the impact on society that *The Exorcist* has had. People began showing up at churches all around the world demanding that an exorcism be performed on them or a loved one. "Demonologists" began to appear out of nowhere, all with dubious knowledge and a price for their services. Many of these were renegade priests and self-proclaimed "holy men." Within weeks of the film's release, reporters began to notice that hospitals were being flooded with patients who had just seen the movie and came in with severe vomiting or hallucinations. Many patients had to be carried out of theaters and driven by ambulance to emergency wards. Newspapers and TV news had a field day. Billy Graham publicly came out and condemned the film, saying that it was "the embodiment of evil." Claims of the devil himself having had a hand in the popularity of the movie reached its climax when the Academy of Motion Picture Arts and Sciences nominated *The Exorcist* for a Best Picture Oscar. No horror film before or since has received that nod.

Some people involved with the film were less dramatic in their thinking regarding a curse. Ellen Burstyn said about the making of the film: "I don't know if it was a jinx, really but there were some really strange goings-on during the making of the film. We were dealing with some really heavy material and you don't fool around with that kind of material without it manifesting in some way." Jason Miller, on the other hand, might feel a bit different. It is said that just prior to filming, Miller was approached by a priest, who asked to speak with him. Miller had never seen the priest before, and the priest had no clue that a film was being shot nearby. According to reports, the priest told Miller that those "who reveal the devil for the trickster that he is, he will seek retribution against you or he will even try to stop what you are trying to do to unmask him." The priest then shook Miller's hand and, without another word, walked away. This, combined with the odd accident involving Miller's son, seems to have convinced the actor that things may have actually been caused by an otherworldly hand.

I will leave it up to my readers to think about all of the strange events that took place before, during and after the making of the film. It is hard to believe that, considering the subject matter, the fact that the story is based on a real possession case and the way the film portrayed the power of evil, the devil himself—if you believe he truly exists—wouldn't at the very least be watching in rapt attention. No matter what one thinks or believes, *The Exorcist* remains known to this day as the scariest horror film ever made.

3
THE CURSE OF *THE CROW*

Do not go ahead with making the movie. If you do, bad things will happen." With this cryptic and anonymous voice message left on the production staff's answering machine on the first day of filming, *The Crow* stepped into movie history and myth. From the very beginning of production, the film was mired in controversy, bad luck and, eventually, death. Many attribute these mishaps to accidents that can and do occur during a long movie shoot. Others say that the mysterious phone call, once ignored, triggered a curse placed by the caller. Still others claim that it was a curse long believed to follow the Lee family after the patriarch flouted Chinese tradition by being buried in a Christian cemetery, next to a small child. Whatever the reason, the curse took its toll on the actors and crew and may still surround the film to this day.

The Crow was based on a comic book about a man, Eric Draven, who is shot and killed after watching his fiancée being brutally beaten and raped. After his funeral, a crow resurrects him to seek revenge on those who committed the crimes. With a dark theme and paranormal overtones, it isn't surprising to find strange things surrounding the film. In keeping with the enigmatic voice message, on the first day of shooting, an accident occurred that almost killed a crew member. According to actor Jon Polito, the worker was using a boom lift to set up lights. He moved the piece of equipment too close to a ditch and fell into it. The operator was pinned under the heavy piece of machinery. When it was lifted to free him, the boom swung into an electrical pole, made contact with the wires and severely electrocuted the man. He caught on fire, but he was quickly extinguished. At the hospital, it was discovered that the man had second- and third-degree burns over half of his body and that all of his internal organs had been burned. The man was only twenty-six years old and had a pregnant wife at home. The crewman eventually recovered but was never the same after this accident. This was just the beginning.

Two days after the boom lift fell into the ditch, the cast and crew were filming a nighttime scene when a prop truck suddenly erupted into flames. By the time the fire was put out, the truck and the props were a total loss. No cause for the fire was ever found. Shortly after this, a stuntman was preparing for a scene when the rooftop set collapsed, causing him to fall through it. The stuntman broke several ribs, one of which came very close to piercing his heart. When he hit the floor, a spike missed going through his head by only a few inches. Following this incident, a carpenter in the arts department slipped on debris on the floor and reached out to steady himself, only to have a screwdriver go all the way through his hand.

It wasn't long after this that a sculptor working in the same arts department drove his car through the set, completely destroying it. There are two versions of this story. Which one is true can now only be guessed at. One states that the sculptor was driving to work at the set and lost control of his car, slamming into a piece of the set. This caused a domino effect that then took out more of the set. The other version of the story—this one much more exciting—comes from the *Los Angeles Times*. In this telling, the sculptor, having been fired from the film, "went berserk" and drove through the set and then through the plaster shop, destroying both in an explosive fit of rage. Whichever theory you choose to believe, the damage was real and set filming back a few weeks.

Accidents aside, the weather in Wilmington, North Carolina, where filming was taking place, seemed to fall prey to the supposed curse as well. Post-production began in the summer of 1993. It is usually hot and humid at that time of year, but in 1993, the weather was anything but predictable. One day would be so humid that the crew needed to make sure the cameras and equipment stayed dry, and the next day would dawn cloudy and cold and saw torrential rains lasting a few days. Then things would go back to horribly hot and muggy. With these sudden changes in weather, many members of the crew came down with ailments that kept them in bed for days. All of this caused delays in the production schedule, which had already been slowed by an earlier death and increased costs. Then, in August 1993, Hurricane Emily hit North Carolina. All work stopped as the storm ripped through the area. The hurricane brought with it record flooding, destructive winds and freezing temperatures. The set was almost completely destroyed. Jon Polito said: "The hurricane was so bad. Of course, we were staying at the Hotel Holiday Inn Cape Fear, so that should give you some sense of what the film was gonna be like." The cast and crew had already begun to think the film was cursed, and some had even contemplated quitting before the curse struck them. But what happened only a few months earlier would stay with everyone involved for the rest of their lives.

With only eight days left in filming, a flashback scene was set be shot. It shows how Draven and his fiancée were killed and how Draven came back from the dead to reap revenge. But due to a bizarre set of circumstances, things went horribly wrong. In this scene, Brandon Lee's character comes into his apartment to find his fiancée being raped and beaten, but before he can do anything, Funboy (Michael Massee) pulls out a .44 handgun and shoots Draven, killing him. The filming seemed to go well. Massee fired, Lee fell to the ground and the director yelled "cut." After the scene was shot, no one knew anything was wrong until someone noticed a growing pool of blood forming around Lee. By the time an ambulance was called, he had lost so much blood that he had to be given immediate transfusions. Unfortunately, the projectile that came out of the barrel of the gun had clipped the stem of the actor's aorta. Brandon Lee passed away on March 31, 1993. What happened that caused this accident?

First, thinking that everything was set for the scene, and needing to scrimp where possible after all of the cost overruns, the weapons master was sent home for the day, and the prop master took over the gun-handling duties. Before Brandon Lee was set to film, a close-up of the .44 pistol was needed, so the gun was loaded with dummy rounds. A dummy round is a bullet that is whole, but there is no gunpowder in the cartridge, so it cannot be fired. After the close-up, the prop master removed the dummy rounds and loaded the gun with blanks. Blanks are the opposite of dummy rounds in that they are loaded with gunpowder but do not have a bullet attached to the cartridge. When a blank is fired, it looks and sounds like an actual round has been fired, but all that comes out of the barrel of the gun is a harmless bit of cotton wadding. Unfortunately, the prop master wasn't trained with firearms and failed to notice that the bullet of the dummy round had come loose and lodged in the barrel of the revolver. When Massee pulled the trigger, the wadding came out of the blank with enough force to cause the dummy round to exit the gun with almost as much velocity as a real bullet. The dummy round then entered Lee's body. Lee underwent surgery to remove the bullet but had lost so much blood from his aorta that he died six hours after being shot.

The rest of the film had to be modified around the death of its star, and one character had to be eliminated completely, as no scenes between this actor and Lee had yet been filmed. The movie was released to mixed reviews. The box office results were adequate but less than expected, which may also be part of the curse. The film did subsequently gain a huge following, but even among these fans is a debate over whether the film or the Lee family itself was cursed.

Brandon Lee came from a long, distinguished Chinese family line. His grandfather Lee Hoi-chuen was a wealthy and influential businessman, and Brandon's father, Bruce Lee, was a movie star and the most famous martial-arts practitioner on the planet. There is some discrepancy about the origins of a Lee family curse. Some claim that Bruce Lee's father had angered a group of Hong Kong merchants. Unable to exact revenge due to Lee's status, they placed a curse on the entire family for as long as there were heirs. Another theory comes from Bruce Lee's brother during an interview he gave shortly after his nephew Brandon's untimely death. "Our father's grave is next to that of a child; this is considered very bad luck in Chinese mythology." It has been suggested that either Hoi-chuen's grave be moved or a wall be erected between his grave and that of the child in order to remove the curse. Neither has yet to be done.

Bruce Lee was born in the Year of the Dragon on the Hour of the Dragon in San Francisco, California. He had an older brother who passed away before Bruce was born. In the Chinese tradition, his parents called Bruce "Little Phoenix," which, when translated into the Chinese language, was a girl's name. This was meant to confuse the demon or entity that was thought to be after the older brother. Bruce knew the tradition and for the rest of his life believed that a demon was after him and, subsequently, his own son. Whether it was a curse, familial bad luck or Bruce's strong belief that brought about a series of strange events, there were definitely some odd coincidences surrounding Bruce and Brandon Lee until their unfortunate deaths.

Bruce Lee died at the age of thirty-three on July 20, 1973, while at the home of his co-star—and some say mistress—Betty Ting Pei. Lee had been complaining about a headache from the moment he got home from the set of *Game of Death*, which ended up being his last film. Pei gave him one of her prescription painkillers, Equagesic. A few hours later, when Betty tried

Although Brandon Lee is buried in Seattle, Washington, many famous Hollywood actors and actresses are interred in Hollywood Forever Cemetery.

to wake Bruce up, he was unresponsive. Instead of calling an ambulance, she called the film's director, who came over, found Lee not breathing and finally called for help. Bruce Lee was pronounced dead at the hospital. The cause of death was cerebral edema caused by an allergic reaction to the painkiller. Lee had been taken to the hospital for the same reason a few months before and had been warned to never take the drug again.

After Lee's death, suspicions ran the gamut, from Betty Pei being hired by the Triad, the Chinese mafia, to rival martial-arts groups jealous of Lee's fame having him killed, to the curse and the demon attached to it finally catching up with Lee and killing him in a martial battle. If it was in fact the curse, it was now free to go after the next in the Lee line: Brandon.

In *Dragon: The Bruce Lee Story*, Lee battles a demon warrior throughout the film. During the final battle, the demon spots Brandon Lee, turns from his battle with Bruce and begins chasing the son. Bruce eventually defeats the cursed warrior, but the film never admits to its total defeat. This symbolic fight may have spread from father to son, as the life of each followed the same odd path. Brandon Lee died in March 1993; his father passed away almost exactly twenty years earlier, in July 1973. Both men died before their last films were released, Brandon of course being killed just prior to the release of *The Crow* and Bruce dying before *Game of Death* was released. *The Crow* was to be Brandon's breakout role, and his performance shows why. Bruce died just a month before his breakout film, *Enter the Dragon*, was to be released. To add to the coincidences, Bruce's character in *Game of Death* is shot while making a movie and comes back to take revenge on those who shot him. Brandon was shot to death while filming *The Crow*. His character was shot and comes back to take revenge on those who killed him. Even though Bruce died from a cerebral hemorrhage, many folks have been swayed by the Mandela effect caused by the similarities of the two movies and believe that both men were shot during filming.

Both men died before filming was complete on their respective movies. Bruce Lee's film was finished with stunt doubles, oblique camera shots and bad special effects. Brandon's movie was finished using stunt doubles and CGI. It is said that Bruce had a premonition of his and his son's deaths. Bruce said after his own father died that he would live to be only half his father's age. His father died at sixty-four; Bruce died at thirty-two. Bruce also stated that he saw that his son would die at a younger age than he would. Brandon died at age twenty-eight.

From the moment *The Crow* was released, it and its sequels have gained cult status, and remakes have been in the works. Every one of them has run into problems with production, location, finances or other aspects. At the time of this writing, another movie is slated to begin filming, but it too seems to be running into trouble. This may be for the better, as I, at least, feel the performance turned in by Brandon Lee will always be the best in this series. Whether you believe in the Lee family curse or that *The Crow* itself was the object of the curse, it is hard to say there wasn't something sinister in the life of the Lee family from the start. *The Crow* may go down as one of the most cursed films of all time.

4

THE MOST CURSED FILM IN HOLLYWOOD

It seems that whenever a movie plot deals with Satan or an evil minion of the devil, especially when the film is a big-budget production, that film inevitably produces a curse. Of course, the content alone may offer a clue as to why this might be the case. Many think it is not a curse. Some believe it is God's wrath for the filmmakers bringing the Evil One into the open, introducing him to the masses, including the weak-minded. Others believe that Lucifer himself is proving that he is the master of chaos, destruction and death, as movies make him out to be. Whatever the case may be, one movie, considered the most cursed in Hollywood history, might involve a bit of both. I am speaking about the cult classic *Rosemary's Baby*.

The reason I say it is possible for both God and the devil to have a hand in the strange and deadly events that surrounded this film since its production was announced is that in *Rosemary's Baby*, Satan is claimed as the victor. The movie also posits that God is dead. This would most likely not be a pleasing concept to the Supreme Being, possibly to the point of awakening His wrath. Satan, on the other hand, to prove that he will be the ultimate victor in the battle between good and evil, might have decided it was a good time to prove this point to those bringing him out of the shadows and into the spotlight. One thing is certain: *Rosemary's Baby* had so many odd things associated with its production and in the years after that it is hard to deny that a supernatural hand might have been in play.

The plot of *Rosemary's Baby* may be passé by today's standards, but in 1968, when it was released, it was both new and terrifying to the point that the Catholic Church denounced it as heretical. The novel, written by Ira

Levin in 1967, tells the story of Guy and Rosemary Woodhouse, a young couple who move into a Gothic but seemingly normal New York apartment building, only to find that the building is occupied by a coven of witches. It isn't long before Rosemary becomes pregnant, which sets into motion a series of strange and frightening events for her. Guy, a struggling actor, meanwhile sees his career skyrocket seemingly overnight. As the story unfolds, it becomes clear that Guy has sold his child to Satan in return for a taste of the fame he has always craved. By the time the film ends, Rosemary has given birth to the Antichrist, God has been relegated to nonexistence and the world is doomed to endure an existence at the hands of evil. It is a plot made for a Hollywood curse.

The curse seems to have reared its ugly head before the film was even a thought in Hollywood's mind. Although the book was widely acclaimed by literary critics as "the best horror novel ever created," "a perfect horror story" and "a modern masterpiece of horror fiction," and despite Levin being hailed as the next Henry James by Truman Capote, Levin himself sank into a state of fear, thinking that his book was blasphemous and would eventually cause him to be blacklisted by publishers and shunned by the media and his readers. Even after producer William Castle bought the movie rights from Levin, the author still couldn't shake his uneasy feeling about the seminal work. Much of Levin's fears came to fruition after the film was released. The Catholic Church called him out publicly for blasphemy, and he was forced to make public statements denouncing Satanism and declaring that he himself was not a Satan worshiper. To make matters worse, his wife left him a year after the film's release for, among other reasons, the toll the notoriety took on their marriage. Levin went out in public less frequently, and he once admitted to Dick Cavett during an interview that he had "become terrified" as he grew older. The book, in essence, ruined his life from the moment it was published.

Producer William Castle was next in line for the curse. Castle was known for his B-grade horror films but had always wanted to produce and direct a big-budget Hollywood horror movie to rival those about Frankenstein and Dracula. He thought he found the perfect script in Levin's novel and immediately bought the movie rights. Castle approached Paramount Studio's Robert Evans about making the film. Evans loved the idea but refused to allow Castle to sit in the director's seat. Instead, Evans decided that a relatively unknown European director, Roman Polanski, was the better choice. Castle had to settle for a producer credit.

After the film's release, furor over the anti-religious aspects of the story, denunciation by almost every religion on the planet and the sheer amount of hate mail Castle received began to take their toll on him. As his stress level grew, Castle's health declined. In April 1969, he developed a severe case of kidney stones, and his kidneys themselves became threatened. Castle was rushed into surgery. Even under anesthesia, he began to dream about and have hallucinations of scenes from the movie. At one point, the doctors were shocked as Castle yelled out from the operating table, "Rosemary, for God's sake drop that knife." Castle did not have another Hollywood hit. William Castle later wrote: "I no longer cared. I was at home, very frightened of *Rosemary's Baby*."

Mia Farrow, who played Rosemary Woodhouse, was not the first choice for the part. She wasn't even the second choice. If she had known what the film would do to her and those she was involved with, she most likely would have turned the part down. Of all those involved, she may have been the luckiest in terms of what the curse doled out. As mentioned, Farrow was not Roman Polanski's first choice; he wanted Tuesday Weld. When Evans flat out refused having Weld in the film, Polanski then pushed for his girlfriend, Sharon Tate. But Evans had already made up his mind that Farrow would play the role of Rosemary. Tate was eventually cast in the film, but only as an extra in an early party scene.

As mentioned, Mia Farrow got off lucky as far as the curse was concerned. Her husband at the time, crooner Frank Sinatra, was asked by Farrow to read the script and give his thoughts on it. After looking it over, Sinatra said, "I can't see you in it." Farrow decided to take the role anyway. At the time, she had already agreed to appear in Sinatra's new movie, *The Detective*, but figured she could split time between both films, even though it meant flying between New York and the West Coast. Unfortunately, the schedule that Polanski set for filming wouldn't allow for that travel time, and Farrow chose *Rosemary's Baby* over her husband's production. Sinatra, angry over her decision, issued an ultimatum: the movie or him. Thinking that Sinatra wouldn't be so rash as to leave her, Farrow continued working on *Rosemary's Baby*. Returning to New York, Farrow was served with divorce papers by Sinatra's lawyer during a filming session. In a state of shock, Farrow signed the papers while crying her eyes out, then went right back to filming. This is the only detrimental thing that happened to Farrow. But those near her, even those not directly involved with the film, were caught up in the curse, with deadly consequences.

Illness, divorce, depression and the termination of careers were just the beginning of this movie's destructive curse. Few of those involved with the film escaped unharmed. The evil involved with this film took its toll in lives lost, some of the circumstances so gruesome that the deaths are forever etched in Hollywood lore and cannot and will not be forgotten. One of the first victims had a striking similarity to a character in the film, and their fate solidifies the curse in the minds of many. Krzysztof Komeda was an up-and-coming composer in the film industry and received praise for the score he created for *Rosemary's Baby*. Shortly after completing his work, Komeda and some friends were having a party on a beach when he slipped and fell down a steep cliff. He suffered a cerebral hemorrhage and slipped into a coma. Komeda languished in the hospital before being sent back to his home country of Poland before passing away. He never regained consciousness. One might consider this a coincidental accident until one realizes how closely Komeda's fate mirrors that of Rosemary Woodhouse's close friend Hutch.

Robert Evans, executive producer of *Rosemary's Baby* and the one who chose Polanski over Castle to direct the film, may have suffered the most under the curse. It didn't kill him, but it made him wish it had. Shortly after *Rosemary's Baby* premiered, Evans's addiction to cocaine began. The producer was still able to function at a high level. In fact, it was during the late 1960s and early '70s that Evans turned Paramount Pictures into one of the most successful and profitable studios in history. He left Paramount in 1974 to produce under his own name. From that point on, both his life and his career took steep downward paths. By 1980, his addiction to cocaine had landed him in jail on a charge of drug trafficking. Evans pleaded guilty to the charge to avoid a long, drawn-out public trial.

Evans's growing drug problem allegedly led him to become involved with a Miami drug cartel and one of its associates, Karen DeLayne Greenberger, aka Elaine "Laynie" Jacobs. Greenberger, who had ties with Colombian cartel boss Carlos Lehder, had dreams of becoming a player in Hollywood. She approached Evans with the idea for a film about the famous 1920s New York nightclub the Cotton Club. Evans brought the idea to fellow producer Roy Radin, who loved the idea. The two men set out to make the movie a reality. Greenberger was offered $50,000 as a finder's fee, which she considered insufficient. She became angry enough to have Radin murdered, and Evans was implicated with her in the killings. During Greenberger's murder trial, Evans was brought up as a witness, but as he pleaded the Fifth on the stand, many considered this an admittance of involvement, further ruining his reputation. After this, Evans's career was virtually over. Robert Evans would go on to have serious health issues, resulting in three strokes. He survived these, but for the rest of his life he had trouble speaking and walking. Everything that occurred in Robert Evans's life following *Rosemary's Baby* could be chalked up

The Dakota apartment building is the Woodhouse's fictional home in the movie *Rosemary's Baby*. It was also where John Lennon lived and was shot and killed. He was a possible victim of the curse.

to bad decisions and were products of his own making. But we must also take into account that they all began after *Rosemary's Baby* was released.

Although Mia Farrow had the least amount of tragedy in her life as a result of the so-called curse, she seems to have passed it on to at least one of her friends, John Lennon. During the Beatles' trip to India in 1967 to study Transcendental Meditation with celebrity guru Maharishi Mahesh Yogi, Farrow was there at the same time for the same reasons. After becoming friends with Lennon during the trip, Farrow was present during many of his recording sessions, and the two came to know each other well. Many of the songs Lennon wrote at the time Mia Farrow was with him in India became part of the band's famous "White Album." In the years after *Rosemary's Baby* was released, Farrow and Lennon kept in touch, until Lennon was gunned down in New York City outside of the iconic 1884 Gothic apartment building, the Dakota. This was the same building Guy and Rosemary Woodhouse move into at the beginning of the cursed film. Lennon happened to be living there when Mark David Chapman caught up to him and put four bullets into his back. Lennon died shortly after the attack. The curse waited twelve years after the film to kill Lennon. But this isn't the only link Lennon had to the fatal curse of *Rosemary's Baby*.

Of all of the tragic things that occurred to those caught up in the curse, none was more brutal and appalling than what happened to the director of *Rosemary's Baby*, Roman Polanski, and his wife, Sharon Tate, who also appeared in the film before they were married. Charles Manson had been listening to the Beatles for years, but when the band's "White Album" came out, he believed, or so he said, that the Fab Four were sending him a message that they were behind his revolution and that it was time to start the race wars he thought would bring about the change he was seeking throughout the United States and possibly the world. He believed that the song "Helter Skelter" from the album had the code words to begin the war. This is one of the songs John Lennon wrote while hanging out with Mia Farrow in India. The words "Helter Skelter" were left in blood at the Cielo Drive murder site to elicit public fear.

Manson intended to use record producer Terry Melcher and his longtime partner, Candice Bergen, as his first sacrificial lambs, but as luck—or the curse—would have it, Melcher had moved out of his rented Cielo Drive ranch house a few months before Manson's planned murder. When Manson sent acolytes Tex Watson, Susan Atkins, Patricia Krenwinkel and Linda Kasabian to the Benedict Canyon home, they found it occupied by Sharon Tate (Polanski) and three of her friends. The four Manson Family members brutally murdered Abigail Folger, Jay Sebring and Wojciech Frykowski by stabbing and shooting. Frykowski was beaten so hard with the butt end of a pistol that the grip shattered. Manson's followers saved Tate, who had appeared in *Rosemary's Baby*, for last. At the time, Tate was tied up, watching her friends being horribly killed. She was more than eight months pregnant and had been pleading with Susan Atkins to let her baby live. In a show of just how callous Manson's followers were to human life, Atkins's response to Tate's pleas was, "Shut up bitch; I don't care about your baby." Atkins then proceeded to stab Tate repeatedly, and when Watson came back, he joined in the massacre. Tate was stabbed sixteen times; her baby received many of the same wounds. Manson's maniacs then used their victims' blood to write "Helter Skelter" on the walls, refrigerator and doors. In all cases, the words were misspelled.

Polanski had left on a business trip to Europe, which is why he wasn't at the house the night of the murders. In an interview, he stated that as he was boarding the plane, a strange thought washed over him, and he couldn't shake it for quite some time. What came to his mind was, "I am never going to see her [Tate] ever again." Could this have been a premonition of the coming murders? Polanski may have avoided being killed, but he was not untouched by the events that took place at his home. After his wife and unborn child were murdered, Polanski sank into a severe depression, which led him down the road of substance abuse and depravity. He began a series of meaningless affairs, some of which were made possible by chemical means. This dangerous and illegal practice led to him fleeing the United States and its justice system. A case against him is still ongoing many decades after his salacious act.

In 1977, Roman Polanski was asked to guest-edit the French edition of *Vogue*. During this time, Polanski met thirteen-year-old Samantha Geimer and convinced her to pose for him in a series of photo shoots. Polanski, using his friendship with Jack Nicholson, coaxed her into going to Nicholson's house for a shoot, where he plied the teenager with champagne laced with narcotics and proceeded to rape her. Polanski was arrested for the sexual assault and spent forty-five days in jail. After posting bail, he fled the country and hasn't again set foot in the United States as of the writing of this book. He has spent the time since then avoiding extradition countries and living the life of a fugitive.

Even though Roman Polanski has never returned to his adopted country and has not visited the graves of his wife and baby son, he has continued to build his career and has become one of the world's foremost directors, achieving fame, fortune and accolades. His life is not unlike that of Guy Woodhouse, who, after sacrificing his wife to the devil, saw his acting career skyrocket. Some believe that Polanski left the country just before the gruesome murders of his wife, unborn son and Tate's friends because he sold them out to Satan. It does seem odd that a man could gain the reputation of master filmmaker, rather than child rapist and fleeing felon, without help from a supernatural power. Of course, when you consider some of the strange celebrities folks choose as their idols, does it really seem so odd that this could also be the case with Polanski?

As with the other films featured in this book, the reader must decide the truth in regards to a curse. Perhaps the strange occurrences surrounding the films are products of coincidence. Whatever the reader decides, the sheer amount of tragedy and death surrounding *Rosemary's Baby* justifies its claim as the most cursed film in Hollywood history to this point.

PART II

PROPHECIES AND PREMONITIONS

5

JAMES DEAN

A RACE TO THE DEATH

Hollywood legends are often conflated with the actors and actresses themselves. Sometimes, the legends are identified with the roles the actors portray, such as Dorothy in *The Wizard of Oz* and Rick in *Casablanca*. And some legends spring up about the films themselves. On rare occasions, it is a combination, such as Rhett Butler and Scarlett O'Hara and the movie *Gone with the Wind*. But Hollywood legends are much more than the films and the characters portrayed in them. Over the decades, as Hollywood has become known as a land of dreams, stories about strange predictions and prophecies of death involving Tinseltown's stars and films have appeared. So many tales exist, in fact, that an entire book could be written about them. Many of these predictions of doom have come from mediums and soothsayers looking for fame, fortune and good standing, but others have come from the stars themselves. And many of these premonitions have unfortunately come true. One of the most well known is in connection with James Dean. In Dean's case, there were two premonitions, as well as an ongoing curse that might have ultimately been the cause of his death.

James Dean, the twenty-four-year-old actor who epitomized 1950s teen angst and coming-of-age characters in movies such as *East of Eden* and *Rebel Without a Cause*, became a legend in his own right. But the legend tag came with a high price: his death. Dean's death has become a legend in Hollywood and beyond.

James Dean was known to love acting and making movies, but his true passion was racing. From the time he watched his first auto race, Dean wanted to become a racecar driver. He dabbled in local races but realized how expensive the sport was. Being of humble origins, Dean lacked the necessary funds to pursue racing as a career. After coming to Hollywood and hitting the big time, Dean knew that his path lay in the film industry, but his passion for racing never diminished. By the time Dean completed filming *East of Eden*, he had the financial resources to afford a good car and enter races throughout California when his schedule allowed. To this end, Dean began looking for a car that would allow him to compete in road and track races. He found the perfect roadster in a brand-new 1955 Porsche Spyder. Dean had traded in the Porsche Speedster he had been driving for the much faster 550 Spyder on September 21, 1955, and promptly entered the upcoming Salinas Road Race, to be held on October 1 and 2. Along with the 550 Porsche, Dean bought a new Ford Country Squire to tow what he now named "Little Bastard."

There is some speculation as to why Dean gave the car this name. Some say that Dean had been given that nickname by Warner Bros. stuntman Bill Hickman, who had become good friends with Dean and joked that Dean was just a little bastard. Dean in turn called Hickman a big bastard. Hickman was part of the entourage heading up to Salinas when Dean left for the road race. Others say that Dean wanted to get back at Warner Bros. head Jack L. Warner. Warner had referred to Dean as a "little bastard" for not vacating the temporary trailer he was using for *East of Eden*. Dean also wanted to get back at Warner for banning him from racing while under a film contract. Naming the car "Little Bastard" was Dean's way of letting Warner know that he was going to race between film projects. This version of the story was corroborated by two of Dean's friends, Lew Bracker and Phil Stern.

The legend of Dean and Little Bastard actually started before Dean purchased the car. On September 17, 1955, four days before he bought the Porsche Spyder, Dean filmed an interview with actor Gig Young for *Warner Bros. Presents* to promote his new movie, *Rebel Without a Cause*. Dean was asked how fast his car could go, and Dean answered, "Oh, 106 or 107 miles an hour." Young then began talking about Dean's racing in Palm Springs and Bakersfield before asking Dean how fast he drove on the highway. Dean replied: "I used to fly around quite a bit, you know, I took a lot of unnecessary chances on the highways. And I started racing and now I drive on the highways and I'm extra cautious. I don't have the urge to speed on the highway. People say racing is dangerous, but I'll take my chances on the track any day [rather] than on the highway." When the interview was almost over, Dean got up to leave. Young asked him one final question: "Do

Although young when he died, James Dean left such a mark on Hollywood that he received his own star at Hollywood and Vine.

you have any special advice for the young people who drive?" Dean looked into the camera and with a bit of a grin said: "Take it easy driving. The life you save might be mine." The driver who helped end Dean's life admitted that he had heard this interview. One might consider Dean's quip a strange coincidence—it may very well have been just that. But when you factor in the bizarre and unsolicited premonition from actor Alec Guinness the first time the two stars met, one might think the Fates were trying to intervene on Dean's behalf.

Alec Guinness and James Dean had never met before September 23, 1955, and their meeting was a simple case of chance and of course Dean wanting to meet a man he admired and learned from while watching his movies. Guinness had just flown to Hollywood for the first time. After a very long flight, according to Guinness, "16 hours at that time and I had been met by Grace Kelly and various people, but found myself alone that evening." Guinness went on to say that a friend of his called him up and said she wanted to take him out to dinner. He said they went to a few upscale restaurants, but because she was wearing trousers, they were not allowed in any of them. They finally ended up a little Italian "dive," but it was completely booked. Guinness said that by that time he would have settled for a hamburger, but as they started to leave, he heard the sound of footsteps running toward them. He said that as he turned, he saw that it was an out-of-breath James Dean who had come up to them. Dean said that he heard they couldn't get a table and asked if they would like to join him. Guinness said that as they were about to enter the restaurant, Dean turned to them and said, "Before we go in, I want to show you my new car."

As Dean took Guinness and his host to the parking lot, Alec Guinness got his first glimpse of Dean's new car. He said that a strange feeling began to come over him. He said that the car was a "little silver, very smart thing all done up in cellophane." Dean had just gotten the car back from having the number *130* painted on the doors, hood and rear in nonpermanent ink and the words *Little Bastard* applied in permanent paint. At the time Dean showed it off to Guinness and his friend, he had never been behind the wheel of the car. Guinness went on to say he asked Dean how fast the car could go. Dean said that he could go "150 in it." Guinness then asked if Dean had driven the car yet, to which Dean said, "No, I've never been in it at all." Guinness recalled what happened next: "Some strange thing came over me, some almost different voice and I said, 'I won't join your table unless you want me too, but I must say something, please do not get into that car, because if you do,' and I looked at my watch, and I said 'if you get into that car at all, it's now Thursday (it was actually Friday),' whatever date it was, 'it's now 10 o'clock at night and by 10 o'clock at night next Thursday, you'll be dead.'" Guinness said they both shrugged it off, had a nice dinner and said they would keep in touch, then went their separate ways. James Dean would be dead before 10:00 p.m. the following Friday, just as Alec Guinness predicted.

On September 30, exactly one week to the day that Dean met Guinness, instead of towing Little Bastard with the Ford Country Squire he bought for that purpose, Dean decided to drive the Porsche Spyder 550 to Salinas in order to get more familiar with its handling and power capabilities before the race. This plan was supported by Porsche mechanic Rolf Wütherich, who kept Dean company as a passenger on the drive from Los Angeles to Salinas. Bill Hickman was following behind the Spyder with a trailer for the return trip. The drive was going great, and everyone was having a good time. The group stopped in Bakersfield for lunch before heading back on the road for the final leg of the journey. Dean decided to open it up on the backroads outside of Bakersfield and was pulled over and issued a speeding ticket. Dean then continued his drive, not slowing down until he reached Route 466 at Route 41 in the city of Paso Robles.

This is the intersection where James Dean's car Little Bastard was struck, killing Dean almost instantly.

At about 5:45 p.m., James Dean and Rolf Wütherich were driving down Highway 466, now Highway 46, at approximately eighty-five miles per hour as they approached the intersection with Highway 41. As they neared, the two men noticed a Ford sedan coming down 41 and not slowing down. Dean turned to Wütherich and told him not to worry, that because the Ford was going to make a left turn it had to stop and give them the right of way. Almost immediately after Dean uttered those words, the Ford Tudor turned left in front of the Porsche Spyder, and the cars collided almost head-on. The impact was brutal. Wütherich was thrown from the sports car and suffered several broken bones and minor internal injuries. The Ford Tudor, driven by twenty-three-year-old Cal-Poly student Donald Turnupseed, was sent almost forty feet down the road. Turnupseed suffered only minor injuries in the horrendous crash. The only fatality was James Dean, the actor who was forewarned of his death exactly one week earlier by Alec Guinness. The man who asked others during an interview to be careful on the road because it might be his life that was saved was killed by Turnupseed, who had watched the interview.

As mentioned earlier, James Dean's death may have been connected to a curse placed on the car before Dean purchased it. More likely, the curse came about as a result of the tragic death of the actor from a violent act. Whichever the case may be, it seems more than likely that the curse of Little Bastard does indeed exist. After the crash, Little Bastard was declared a total loss by the insurance company and was taken to a salvage yard in Burbank, California. Dr. William F. Eschrich, another racer who had competed against Dean on a couple of occasions, purchased the wrecked car to strip it for parts, some to be used in his Lotus IX race car and others to be sold. During Eschrich's next race, while using the engine from Little Bastard, his Lotus crashed into the wall at Pomona Raceway. Eschrich was injured but survived the crash, but another driver wasn't so lucky.

During that race, Troy McHenry was also driving a car using parts from Little Bastard. McHenry was friends with Eschrich, who had loaned him the transmission and suspension from the Porsche Spyder. Just before the race, McHenry was seen adjusting the steering on his Porsche 550 and seemed satisfied with the results. But on the first lap, in one of the turns, McHenry's car began to shimmy. He motioned to his crew that he had no steering. He lost control, and the car slammed into the only tree on the raceway, killing McHenry instantly.

After Eschrich was finished with the car, Little Bastard was sold to George Barris, the self-proclaimed "King of the Kustoms." Barris promised

A memorial sign now stands at the intersection where James Dean lost his life.

to rebuild the iconic car, but the mangled frame made that impossible. Barris loaned the car to the Los Angeles chapter of the National Safety Council from 1957 to 1959, after which it was stored in a garage in Fresno, California. While there, Little Bastard mysteriously caught fire. Two of the car's tires burned, and the paint was scorched at the words *Little Bastard*. Other than that, no damage was done, and none of the other cars in the garage were touched by the flames. Other strange and alarming things happened around Little Bastard. A driver who had bought the two remaining tires was injured when both tires blew out simultaneously in the car he was driving. During its time with the National Safety Council, the body of the car mysteriously kept falling off its display stand. The car once fell off the trailer as it was being transported. Truck driver George Barkus was killed. Then, while being transported from Miami to Los Angeles, Little Bastard mysteriously disappeared.

Over the years, folks have claimed to find parts of Little Bastard all over the country. The car may have been disassembled, crated and spread far and wide. Many believe this was done to make sure the curse of Little Bastard would no longer hurt anyone. Supposed parts of the Porsche Spyder have shown up, but only one has ever been confirmed as being an original piece of Dean's car: a transaxle found in a wooden crate in

Massachusetts. Other than that, the rest of Little Bastard has not been seen since its disappearance in 1960.

Believe what you want about Little Bastard and its curse. Maybe Dean was caught up in the curse of the car. Or perhaps he was the cause of it. Whatever one thinks about the story of Dean's untimely death and his car, one thing is certain. When you take into account Dean's last interview, the premonition uttered by Guinness a week before Dean's death and the odd things involved with Little Bastard, there was nothing normal about the death of the young man who had such a bright future ahead of him.

6

OLIVER REED

A DRINK TO DIE FOR

Oliver Reed never intended to become an actor. As a matter of fact, he decided to give it a try one night while out drinking with friends who just happened to be working as film extras. Once Reed gave it a try, he not only liked the challenge of it, but he also found he was good at it and decided to make acting his career. Reed had always been a hard drinker, and being in films didn't change that. He may have slowed down a bit to work on his craft, but once the camera stopped rolling, Reed could usually be found in a pub, having a few pints with friends and enjoying his time off the set.

Reed portrayed numerous hard-charging, stubborn, stern and malcontented characters, many of whom have become Hollywood icons. His portrayal of Athos in the 1973 remake of *The Three Musketeers* and 1974's *The Four Musketeers* solidified him as the epitome of that characterization. His work in *Burnt Offerings*, *The Brood*, *Crossed Swords* and *The Adventures of Baron Munchausen* showed his range and ability to perform in both adventure films and comedies. Perhaps his best-known role, and also his last, was that of Proximo, the former gladiator and slave turned owner of slaves in *Gladiator*.

It was during the filming of this movie that Oliver Reed died from a heart attack while in a bar in Valletta, Malta, in 1999. Heart attacks are not uncommon, and Reed's was no different. What was unusual in this case was the fact that Reed predicted his own death years before it occurred. Not only did he make this prediction, but it also was so close to the actual event that there is little doubt that some paranormal force was at work, telling him subconsciously what his fate would be.

In 1993, Oliver Reed appeared on the British television show *Without Walls: The Obituary Show*. This pseudo-documentary series featured living people speaking into the camera supposedly from beyond the grave, telling the audience how they died. As strange as this show was, it had a devoted fan base. The show wasn't on the air long, but the episode featuring Reed is one that will be watched for a very long time. (It can be found on YouTube.) Reed told the audience: "I died in a bar of a heart attack full of laughter. We were having a cabbage competition. I was very confident that for once I was going to win this vegetable competition. And somebody made a bet with me that was so lewd that I took it on and he shook my hand. And I laughed so much I was sick and died." Reed died six years later, and his invented tale about his death for the most part matched his actual death.

By 1999, Reed's career had hit rock bottom. During the '90s, he appeared in only a couple of films and was better known for his many inebriated TV appearances. *Gladiator* was to be his comeback movie. Because of this, he hadn't had a single drink for months before filming began. That all changed on May 2, 1999, when Reed, his wife and a few friends headed into the city of Valletta, Malta, during a break in filming and ended up in an Irish bar simply named The Pub. Details about how much alcohol Reed consumed

Oliver Reed was a favorite on the big screen, and his performances may have been shown at the posh Warner Pacific movie palace on Hollywood Boulevard before it closed down.

that night are sketchy, but one report said that he consumed "three bottles of Captain Morgan's Jamaican rum, eight bottles of German beer, numerous doubles of Famous Grouse whiskey and Hennessy cognac." It also said that he left a bar tab of $600. While at The Pub, Reed, infused with copious amounts of liquor, began arm-wrestling with the many British navy sailors who frequented the bar, beating most of them. At one point, Reed decided to pick up the tab for the entire bar.

All of the alcohol, mixed with physical activity and his age, was too much for Reed's body to handle. Reed gave a laugh and dropped dead from a heart attack. The only thing missing was the cabbage. One of his friends, who, according to the *Irish Times*, did not want to be identified, told the paper: "He had been drinking on the floor when he felt sick. I tried giving him artificial respiration on a bench as an ambulance was called." Unfortunately, by the time Reed's friend began CPR, it was too late. Oliver Reed was dead. There is an urban legend that Reed predicted not only his death but also what would be written on his tombstone. In *Without Walls*, he quipped, "My tombstone will read, 'He made the air move.'" How the legend of this prediction came about is unknown, but this seems like a strange myth, as Reed's statement on the show was likely the reason these words were carved into his tombstone.

Reed appeared in more than ninety films, but the closest he came to winning an Oscar was when the film *Oliver!* won for Best Picture and Reed received praise for his portrayal of the menacing Bill Sikes. As talented as Oliver Reed was, he received just one acting award while alive. At Fantafestival in 1983, he won the Best Actor Award for his work in *Dr. Heckyl and Mr. Hype*. He was a nominee in 1991 for Best Performance by an Actor in a Supporting role in a Movie or Miniseries at the CableACE Awards. Reed died before the movie *Gladiator* was completed, and this forced director Ridley Scott to finish Reed's scenes using a combination of a double and digital outtake footage. Nevertheless, the film was dedicated to his memory, and Reed was the BAFTA Awards nominee for Best Actor in a Supporting Role in 2000, posthumously, of course. He failed to win the award. Reed gave us so much pleasure from his many movie roles, and those memories will stay with us. Unfortunately, he is now known more for his strangely accurate prediction of his own death than for his incredible acting ability.

7

SHARON TATE, JAY SEBRING, PREMONITIONS AND MURDER

Sharon Tate, despite having been an up-and-coming actress, is most known for her violent murder. Tate was a victim of one of the most horrific mass murders in history when, on the night of August 9, 1969, Tate and three of her friends, along with Steven Parent, a young man visiting a friend in the guest house at 10050 Cielo Drive, were brutally murdered by members of the Manson Family in an attempt to start a race war between Blacks and whites in the belief that African Americans would win the war but be unable to run the planet without the help of Manson and his Family. To this day, the Manson Murders, as they have come to be called, stand out in the annals of true crime as one of the most brutal assaults in American history. One of the strange tales related to this heinous crime involves the theory that Tate may have been warned of her death by a prophetic dream that should have been taken more seriously than it was.

Three years before the killings, Sharon Tate was between apartments and needed a place to stay for a couple of days. She had previously dated Jay Sebring and asked if she could stay with him until she found a place of her own. Sebring's house, in Benedict Canyon, had once belonged to Jean Harlow and Paul Bern. It was also where Bern committed suicide—at least the official cause of death was suicide. Jay Sebring's new home was less than a mile from where Sharon Tate would be murdered. Sebring was on a business trip, so Tate was alone in the house. She told friends that she had been getting a strange vibe all night but figured it was just her imagination, a result of being alone in a strange house. She tried to put it out of her

The mansion shown here finally replaced the ranch house where Sharan Tate, Jay Sebring and others were brutally murdered by Charles Manson's followers.

mind. She was lying in bed, trying to fall asleep. She left a light on next to the bed to help keep the vibe at bay. Tate suddenly noticed a "creepy little man" enter her bedroom. She recognized him from Sebring's photos as the previous owner. She knew she was looking at Paul Bern and that he seemed to be looking for something. Tate had no idea what it could be, but she wasn't about to wait to find out. Tate grabbed her robe, dashed for the bedroom door and made her way down the stairs. At the bottom, she immediately wished she had stayed in her room, because what greeted her was something out of a horror movie. There in front of her was a person. She couldn't tell if they were male or female, but she saw they were tied to the staircase and their throat had been slit open. Tate began to suspect that she was either still in bed and dreaming or she was seeing visions. The vision had no real form or solidity. In either case, Tate was now almost in a panic and needed a drink. She didn't know where Jay kept the liquor, but something in her mind told her to open the bookcase. She didn't know where the thought had come from, but when she opened the bookcase, she found a hidden bar and promptly poured herself a drink.

As she slowly sipped the alcohol, she noticed some strange wallpaper and began to pick at it until she uncovered the beautiful copper base to the bar. Again, thinking she must be dreaming, she retraced her steps, past the body tied to the railing and past the ghost of Paul Bern. Tate somehow managed to go back to sleep. The next morning turned out to be a beautiful day, and when Tate woke up, everything she had seen the night before was still fresh in her mind. She kept telling herself that it had only been a dream; she had not seen a ghost or any of the other visions she thought she saw. As she got out of bed, she heard Jay Sebring come through the front door. Before she had a chance to head down the stairs and tell him what had happened during the night, she heard him call up: "Hey, who tore the wallpaper off the bar down here?"

That's when Sharon Tate realized it had not been a dream. Almost exactly three years later, Tate and Sebring were tied together with ropes, just as she had envisioned. They were stabbed and killed, just as the apparition had been. And it took place just a mile from where Tate had her visions. Could this have been Paul Bern's way of trying to warn Tate of the danger that awaited her? Could this have been her own precognitive ability, manifesting itself in an effort to save her? Or was it just a cosmic coincidence? Unfortunately, we will never know.

Many stories of the paranormal in regards to the Manson killings and Sharon Tate come from the home of David Oman. Oman lives on Cielo Drive, five houses down from where Sharon Tate, Jay Sebring and three others were killed. Not long after Oman moved into his house, he began to notice strange things happening inside the home. At one point, he thought he saw someone in his house and initially thought it was a burglar or other intruder. He soon realized that what he saw was wispy and insubstantial. He began to realize they may be spirits, but who these spirits could be he didn't know. He decided to do a bit of research into his home's history and found a picture of Jay Sebring, whom he recognized as the person he had been seeing in the house. Oman then realized that what he had been witnessing were the spirits of the murder victims from the home just up the street. Over the years, he discovered that it was not just Sebring who was trying to make himself known, but Sharon Tate as well. It would seem that Sebring and Tate had unfinished business. Or they may have been trying to ensure that they were not forgotten. They may have wanted people to remember them as they were in life, with all of their accomplishments, and not as murder victims.

Oman is not shy about letting people know that his home is haunted. He has openly embraced the spirits as honored guests and has even given them an outlet for bringing their message to the public. Oman has opened his house to people who have a desire to investigate the unknown, and his

Sharan Tate was pregnant at the time she was killed. Her baby received many of the same stab wounds as did his mother.

property has never failed to give these adventurers what they seek. Renowned paranormalist Dr. Barry Taff, who became famous for his investigations of the "Entity" case, was the first to document the activity in the home. He has recorded so much activity that he has nicknamed the house the "Mount Everest of haunted houses" and "Disneyland for the dead."

Oman has never worried about the "spirited" visitors who appear in his home. He views them as guests and once said: "I always felt that I wasn't alone here....I'm way more scared of the living than the dead." Those who have participated in tours of the house report that Taff and Oman have not overstated the nicknames for the home. I truly believe that the spirits are thankful to have a place where they and the evils that took their lives can be remembered in the hopes that we can keep them from happening in the future.

Sharon Tate, Jay Sebring and Paul Bern will always be linked by tragedy and mystery. We know what happened to Tate while staying in the house once owned by Bern and his wife, Jean Harlow. Bern appeared to Tate in what has been called a spiritual intervention, a warning about her impending demise. It appears that Bern may have also been trying to warn Sebring of his impending death at the hands of Manson.

It seems that Jay Sebring began to feel uneasy in his home after the strange incident Sharon Tate experienced while staying in the Bern/Harlow house.

Sebring began to make excuses to stay out later than he normally would when visiting friends and family. He also extended his business trips and took more time away from home than usual. He told his confidants that when he was in the house, especially alone, he would get the feeling that he was being watched and of never actually being alone. Sebring brought a medium into the home a few months before the fateful night in August 1969. She told him that someone was telling her of his death "in a house with bare beams visible in the ceiling" and described Sebring as being shot and stabbed to death in a horrific act of murder. This unverified urban legend goes on to say that Sebring, believing that his home, which had visible ceiling beams, was where he would be killed, began to take even more time away, to the point of almost never being there. It never dawned on him that the home of his former girlfriend, Sharon Tate, had the same exposed beams, even more, than the Bern/Harlow house. Sebring was butchered shortly after the medium's warning. Could Bern have been speaking through the medium to warn Sebring, as he had Tate?

Bern may have warned Tate and Sebring about their impending doom, but why would he have stayed in the house? And why would he have cared what happened to others? The story of Paul Bern and his death may seem simple, but it has twists and turns of its own and may be a case of murder, rather than the suicide history claims it to be.

Paul Bern was a prominent MGM movie producer and Hollywood insider who knew how to assess talent. This may be one of the reasons why Jean Harlow, one of the most beautiful women to grace the silver screen, fell in love and married Bern. Many in Hollywood at the time couldn't figure out what Harlow saw in Bern, who was twice her age and not a very attractive man. Many believe that the twenty-two-year-old Harlow became enamored with the older Bern because he was the one who not only took a chance on her career but also knew she could act and believed in her. Whatever the reason, Bern and Harlow wed on July 2, 1932. But Bern wasn't aware that by marrying Harlow, her freeloading mother came with her and would put a strain on the marriage from the beginning. As happy as the couple seemed, at least outwardly, Paul Bern committed suicide just over two months after their nuptials. Or did he?

Early in the morning of September 5, 1932, the phone rang at MGM's head office. Paul Bern's frantic butler told the executive who responded to the call that Bern was dead. The butler had found Bern in the bathtub, nude, a bullet hole in his head and a .38 pistol still in his hand—the apparent victim of suicide. This is the official story and the documented cause of death on Bern's death certificate. Although Harlow, MGM and Bern's sister did not dispute this determination, some believe a massive cover-up was performed by MGM, the mob or perhaps both in order to keep Jean Harlow's reputation from suffering and thereby keeping her movie profits coming in for the studio and for Harlow's mother.

By now it is well known that Paul Bern kept a secret from almost everyone in his life: he was married to Dorothy Millette at the time he exchanged vows with Jean Harlow. But there is growing evidence from newspaper articles of the time and Bern's sister's account that Bern was never officially married to Millette but that she was a common-law wife. Even that is disputed, as they hadn't actually lived together long enough for it to be a legal common-law marriage. One theory has been put forth that Millette, finding out that Bern removed her from his will and replaced her with Harlow, drove Millette to kill Bern in an act of defiance. Millette was reportedly seen at Bern's home the night before the suicide, and she was seen two days after his death boarding the *Delta King* riverboat on September 6. She was not seen leaving the ship, and Millette's body was finally found washed up on the shore of the Sacramento River by two fishermen near Walnut Grove. Millette's death, like Bern's, was ruled a suicide.

Psychic medium Ann Bender claims to have made contact with the spirit of Dorothy Millette, who told her that she did not kill Paul but had herself been murdered by Jean Harlow's mother through her husband's mob connections. Millette then went on to tell Bender that MGM, hoping to cover up any connection to Harlow, hired one of its actresses, who resembled Millette, and had her board the *Delta King*. She made herself visible enough so that everyone thought Millette was actually on board. She then removed her makeup, wig and clothing, leading to the assumption that Millette had disappeared from the ship. Millette said her body had already been placed in the Sacramento River before the *Delta King* sailed, thereby making it look as if she, wracked with guilt over murdering her husband, committed suicide. It is well known that Harlow's mother, Jean (Harlow took her mother's name as her stage name), had deep ties to the mob through her husband, who was part of the inner circle of the Mafia's Pacific Coast cartel.

Another theory floating about is that personnel at MGM, having been the first called after the murder and some of whom had been at Bern's house hours before the police were notified, knew about Millette, knew that she had murdered Bern and instituted an elaborate plan to keep Harlow's image free from scandal. It is said that not only did the studio murder Millette at Bern's home but also had taken her body to the Sacramento River, thus completing

David Oman's residence is only five houses from 10050 Cielo Drive.

the narrative just described. This theory goes on to say that MGM also wrote Bern's suicide note and made up a story about Bern having problems of a sexual nature and having a small penis—these were provided as reasons Bern supposedly killed himself. We may never know what really happened to Paul Bern the night he died. What we do know is that Bern was shot in the head, either by his own hand or, as many believe, by someone else.

Considering the nature of what happened in September 1932 in the house and those connected with it, this tragedy may be why Paul Bern is still there. And if, as many believe, he didn't take his own life, he may have tried, with his warnings to Tate and Sebring, to let others know he was murdered and to spare them the same fate. This behavior matches Bern's while he was alive. He was well known to others at MGM as someone they could go to for advice, solace or a talk, with the knowledge that it would stay between Bern and those who confided in him.

No one deserves the brutal treatment that befell Sharon Tate, Jay Sebring, the other Cielo Drive victims and perhaps Paul Bern. This kind of tragedy will leave a mark on one's soul that may never be washed away and may keep the spirit of the one wronged bound to this mortal realm in the hopes that one day their story will be known and they can pass on into the light of eternity.

8

CARRIE FISHER AND THE FORCE

Carrie Fisher is best known for playing Princess Leia Organa in the *Star Wars* films. As the daughter of actress Debbie Reynolds, she was destined to have a long career in movies and television. Fisher appeared in over eighty-five films and television shows, and she had a successful career as a screenwriter and novelist. But she will always be defined by her portrayal of the tough, intelligent and beautiful Princess Leia in perhaps the most popular film series of all time.

Fame has a way of catching folks unawares, and the stress of that fame can lead down dark roads. This was the case with Fisher, as it has been for so many others who have begun acting at a young age or are the child of a famous parent, or both. Carrie Fisher began using drugs as a young woman and battled her addiction for the rest of her life. She was known to experience mental illness, either due to drug use or exacerbated by it. But in combination, these two factors would have a lasting and telling influence over her life until the day she died.

According to Fisher's daughter, Billie Lourd, her mother never shied away from talking about her addiction. Her daughter said, "My mom battled drug addiction and mental illness all of her life. She ultimately died of it. She was purposefully open in all of her work about the social stigmas surrounding these diseases. She talked about the shame that torments people and their families confronted by these diseases. I know my mom, she'd want her death to encourage people to be open about their struggles. Seek help, fight for government funding for mental health programs. Shame and those social stigmas are the enemies of progress....Love you, Momby."

Carrie Fisher was flying home to Los Angeles from London on December 23, 2016, when, shortly before her plane landed, a passenger seated nearby noticed that she wasn't breathing. Another passenger performed CPR, and the plane made an emergency landing. Paramedics transported her to UCLA Medical Center. It was determined that Fisher had gone into cardiac arrest and was sent to the intensive care unit. For four days, she lay in bed on a ventilator but never regained consciousness. She passed away at the age of sixty on December 27, 2016. Her daughter confirmed her mother's passing later that day.

Fisher had a huge and devoted fan base, and the news of her death hit them hard. It took twelve days for the coroner to issue a death certificate, and the report stunned her fans. The medical examiners found that Fisher died from myocardial infarction but listed "sleep apnea and other factors" as contributors. Fisher also suffered from atherosclerotic heart disease. In this condition, fats and cholesterol build up on the artery walls, putting a strain on the heart. Those facts alone were not what bothered Carrie Fisher's fans; it was the statement in the report saying there were signs of "multiple drug intake" but that the significance of these on Fisher's death could not be determined. Most of her fans knew about her past drug use, but they believed it was in her past and were taken aback to find out that she may have still been using.

The inimitable Princess Leia was Fisher's breakout role, but it was the Force that was the star of the films. Call it magic, sorcery or the essence of life, the Force was an invisible power that was the catalyst for everything in the plots of the movies. As her character became one of the foremost practitioners of this power, Fisher made us all believe that the Force might indeed exist. Fisher may have believed that the power was alive in her own life, or, at the very least, a hidden ability she and those around her didn't know she possessed. Carrie Fisher predicted her own death thirteen years before it happened.

Singer-songwriter James Blunt was a close friend of Carrie Fisher. He called her his "American mother." Blunt was staying at Fisher's home in Los Angeles while working on his album *Back to Bedlam* when he received a strange offering from Fisher that was left outside his door. Blunt once said that he gave this album its name because "I lived in a madhouse with her." He wrote his top 10 hit "Goodbye My Lover" on a piano in Fisher's home. Blunt said that one day as he was leaving his room, he noticed a full cardboard cutout of Fisher as Princess Leia outside his door. Thinking this a strange gift, he found it even more odd that, written across Leia's forehead

Carrie Fisher is buried in a prominent place at Forest Lawn Cemetery.

Debbie Reynolds, Carrie Fisher's mother, died just one day after her daughter.

in Fisher's handwriting was the date of her birth and, underneath that, the date of her death.

During an interview with the *Sunday Times*, Blunt said, "I'm trying to remember what the exact date was, because it was around now and I remember thinking it was too soon. She went out with a bang, as she was back in movies. Maybe it was a great time to go." Blunt and Fisher were so close that Blunt made Carrie Fisher the godmother of his son. In the interview, he stated, "The saddest thing is that my son will never get to know someone I thought was the most special person. Fisher was my American mother and a real inspiration."

Maybe it was the fact that Blunt and Fisher were so close that she decided to give him the warning from her premonition, or perhaps he was just convenient due to his living in her house at the time. But it seems like an odd coincidence that, if it was indeed a premonition of her own death, it came at a time when someone thought of as family would be living with her. Whatever the truth may be, the date of Carrie Fisher's death was so close to the date she wrote down on the cardboard cutout that it is hard to believe it is a coincidence. It seems she was a lot closer to her Princess Leia character than even she may have believed and that the Force actually was with her, at least this one time.

JOHN LENNON AND THE NUMBER 9

John Lennon is known for his music, his ideals of peace and harmony and, of course, for being in perhaps the most successful music group of all time, The Beatles. Not many folks associate John Lennon and Hollywood, and that is to be expected, as Lennon was primarily a singer and songwriter. But John Lennon has a closer connection to Hollywood than many people realize. He appeared in numerous movies, such as *Help!*, *A Hard Day's Night* and *Yellow Submarine*. Although these films were produced and filmed in England, many believe them to be Hollywood productions. The closest connection to Tinseltown that Lennon had, however, is not due to his music or his films, but for a string of murders that John had nothing to do with but to which he had an unwitting, tenuous connection. These were the Manson Family's murders of Sharon Tate and others.

John Winston Lennon was born on October 9, 1940, in Liverpool, England. He grew up in his aunt's home, where she taught him to play the banjo. Even though John's mother was not living with him, she visited often, and they stayed close. John was devastated when his mother was fatally killed by an off-duty police officer who struck her car in 1958. After picking up the banjo and realizing he had a knack for it, he began experimenting with the guitar. He found this much more to his liking and dove headfirst into perfecting his skills with the instrument. While learning the guitar, he also began writing songs and putting music to his lyrics. It wasn't long before he formed his own band, The Quarrymen.

Lennon met Paul McCartney in July 1957 and invited him to join his group. In turn, Paul introduced John to George Harrison. The three finally decided on Pete Best as their drummer and began playing in clubs all over England and Germany. The first song The Quarrymen recorded was a cover of Buddy Holly's "That'll Be the Day." Lennon, being a fan of Buddy Holly and the Crickets, said that it was Holly who inspired him to rename the group. John once said that he had a vision when he was twelve years old of a man appearing to him on a flaming pie who told him, "From this day on, you are Beatles with an 'a.'"

When the Beatles were discovered by Brian Epstein in 1961 and he became their new manager, Epstein thought that Pete Best didn't fit with the other members. So, he basically pushed him out. Epstein brought in Richard Starkey to replace Best. Starkey was an oddball character who fit in perfectly with the quirky personalities of Lennon, McCartney and Harrison. Starkey, known as Ringo Starr, became the fourth member of the Fab Four.

The Beatles would go on to become perhaps the most successful music group of all time. Crowds flocked to see them play, with whole stadiums filled beyond capacity and tickets selling out within minutes of going on sale. After they appeared on *The Ed Sullivan Show*, fans in the United States became just as fanatical as those in England and Europe. Young girls and women worked themselves into frenzies as the Beatles drove down streets or entered hotels, theaters or sold-out stadiums. Many fans passed out from sheer excitement. Even a few men passed out. It was "Beatlemania," and it was The Beatles coming to America that helped coin the phrase "British Invasion" in regards to English rock groups that followed.

Like all good things, even the Beatles had to end. The band gave up touring after their concert at Candlestick Park in San Francisco in 1966. They headed back to the studio to record "Penny Lane / Strawberry Fields Forever," followed by the album *Sgt. Pepper's Lonely Hearts Club Band* in 1967. The death of Brian Epstein from an accidental overdose of sleeping pills hit the band hard, but they managed to complete their film *Magical Mystery Tour*, which included the cryptic song "I Am the Walrus." Following the release of their last film, *Yellow Submarine*, the Beatles released the album *The Beatles*, otherwise known as the "White Album." This, of all their albums, would have the most profound impact on the world when Charles Manson co-opted and used its songs and the band as the catalyst for the start of an intended race war. This was to be initiated by killing Sharon Tate and others in the most brutal ways imaginable. Manson used the song "Helter Skelter" to claim that The Beatles were in fact on his side of the race war and that the song was proof of their backing. The group officially broke up in September 1969, just after completing *Abbey Road*, but news of the breakup wasn't announced until April 1970. The Beatles were at an end.

John Lennon went on to have a mediocre solo career, although it was not always as a solo artist. John and his wife, Yoko Ono, formed the Plastic Ono Band. Despite many famed musicians being featured in the group—Eric Clapton, Keith Moon and even Starr and Harrison—the Plastic Ono Band never caught on with audiences. The group disbanded in 1974. Lennon did have a few hit singles, namely "Give Peace a Chance" and the song he is now most known for, "Imagine." But he never achieved anything close to the success he had as a Beatle. After Ono gave birth to John's second son, Sean, Lennon retired from the music business to focus on being a husband and father. Even though he had officially left the limelight, his fans remained loyal, even after his death in 1980.

Lennon returned to music in 1980 with his album *Double Fantasy*. But only a few weeks after its release, Mark David Chapman, a deranged fan, shot and killed Lennon in front of his apartment building, the Dakota—the same building used in the film *Rosemary's Baby*. As Lennon arrived home on the evening of December 8 to say goodnight to his son, as he was about to ascend the stairs, five shots rang out. One bullet missed its mark completely, but four others struck Lennon, who barely managed to crawl to the doorman before collapsing. Even though Chapman was a big fan of Lennon's, he planned the murder a couple of month earlier after seeing an interview Lennon gave in 1966 in which he quipped, "We're bigger than Jesus now." Chapman was also angered by Lennon professing "love and peace" while living a lavish lifestyle that seemed to contradict his songs. Chapman was also influenced by J.D. Salinger's character Holden Caulfield in the book *The Catcher in the Rye*, who despised the hypocrisy of adults. Chapman said, "I felt by killing John Lennon, I would become somebody." Chapman was sentenced to between twenty years and life for second-degree murder under an insanity plea.

John Lennon had always been a spiritual person, and he made many predictions that came true, despite not intending his words to actually be predictions. One of these may have been a premonition of his death. Lennon may have unknowingly hinted at his own demise on more than one occasion. As far back as 1965, during a press conference in Detroit, Lennon was asked, "Is it true The Beatles are leaving show business in a year?" Lennon responded, "No, we'll either go in a plane crash or we'll get popped off by some loony." Many think this was just another of the offbeat,

John Lennon may not have been officially "Hollywood," but with a star at Hollywood and Vine, it is hard to deny his place in Tinseltown.

irreverent comments by a man who was known to have a full but odd sense of humor. But when one considers that Lennon died in the latter situation, by a loony, it makes one wonder.

John Lennon's first wife, Cynthia, in her book *John*, wrote that after John began overusing LSD, he sometimes forgot who he was and went into an odd sort of trance. During one of these incidents, John blurted out, "They are going to shoot me, you know." Another time that he may have predicted his own death while high on LSD came near the end of the line for The Beatles. Lennon called the other three members into the studio and told them, "I am Jesus and they are going to kill me. But I've got at least four more years to go, so I've got to do stuff." When Ringo heard John say he was Jesus, Ringo simply said, "Ah, ok, meeting is over," and they left John sitting alone in the room.

In other cases, John's premonitions came about in his music. The Beatles' *Abbey Road*, one of the last albums released by the group, includes the song "Come Together." If you listen closely to the song, you will hear John whisper, "shoot me" at the beginning of the song and more than once throughout. The song "Happiness Is a Warm Gun," recorded on the "White Album," is a departure for the band and Lennon. Some fans wonder why it was ever written—other than, of course, as a premonition of things to come. Lennon's last prediction may be on his last album, which was released posthumously and included the song "Borrowed Time." One of the lyrics comes across as perhaps an eerie look at the state of Lennon's mind just before his death: "Living on borrowed time, without a thought for tomorrow."

Lennon wasn't the only one predicting how he would meet his end. In her book, Cynthia Lennon said that they were constantly getting messages from psychics beginning in 1965 warning John about his impending doom. She said that many of these predictions were dismissed as coming from charlatans. But others were much more believable and many quite worrisome. According to the book, psychics began to claim that "John would be shot while he was in the States." She went on to say that these predictions became so common that "when John left on tour [to America] he was frightened and downcast." Lennon's former wife went on to say that the predictions continued right up until December 1980, when he was shot and killed in the States.

Premonitions aside, it seems that Lennon was always surrounded by the supernatural, or at the very least a force we can't define. In numerology, the number 9 represents "completion but not finality. The ending of one cycle and the potential it creates for another to begin." This seems to fit well with the ever-changing life cycles that John Lennon went through during his life and may be the reason that this number was such an important part of his life. The number 9 came up so often that it could no longer, for Lennon or Cynthia, be claimed as a coincidence. The number had been a part of John's life from the day he was born until the day he died. Cynthia Lennon once said that 9 came up so often that both she and John found it strange and sometimes scary.

John Lennon was born on October 9, 1940. His second son, Sean, was also born on October 9. John's first home when he was growing up was 9 Newcastle Road. This is only the beginning of the saga of John Lennon and the number 9. On June, 9, 1957, Lennon's first band, The Quarrymen, entered a contest at Liverpool's City Center. In the audience sat agent and star-maker Carroll Levis. Levis had traveled from London seeking undiscovered talent for his show *Search for the Stars*. Lennon's group didn't win the contest, but the defeat hit the band so hard that they recommitted to the perfection of their music and showmanship, and they became one of the most sought-after independent bands in England. After perfecting their sound and performance, the group, now known as The Beatles, began playing at the Cavern Club and became a staple at the underground venue. The Beatles became so popular that those coming to the club began spreading the word that this was "the greatest band" in Liverpool. Their first day on stage at the Cavern Club was February 9, 1961. Then, on November 9, 1961, Brian Epstein made a reservation to see The Beatles at the club. After seeing them play, he officially became their manager in December, and The Beatles were about to make history.

Now that The Beatles were making a splash all over Europe with their new sound, Epstein decided it was time to introduce the boys to America. To get a large audience of viewers, Epstein worked to have the band appear on *The Ed Sullivan Show*. On February 9, 1964, The Beatles performed their hits "All My Loving," "She Loves You" and "I Saw Her Standing There" before the largest audience to watch a TV show up to that time. After the show, Beatlemania gripped the United States. After they performed at Carnegie Hall on the same trip, the Fab Four was born.

It wasn't only Lennon's professional life that the number 9 seems to have influenced. John met Cynthia on May 9, 1958, but didn't start dating her until the following autumn. Cynthia broke off her engagement to another man to be with John, and John broke off his relationship to be with her. The two were finally married in 1962 after Cynthia became pregnant with their son, Julian. Cynthia later said that when she and John met, she was living at house number 18. She said that John always told her that since 18 is 9

It is fitting that John Lennon's star is next to that of one of his idols, Buddy Holly.

times 2, they were destined to be together. Julian was born in room 126 in the hospital. To John, the fact that the three numbers add up to 9 was a good omen for their son.

In November 1966, John Lennon attended the opening of an exhibit by avant-garde artist Yoko Ono. During the event, Lennon asked if he could hammer a nail into a piece titled "Hammer a Nail." As the exhibit wouldn't be open for another hour, Ono refused. Lennon then told her, "I'll give you an imaginary five shillings and hammer in an imaginary nail." Yoko, obviously amused, climbed up the ladder, wrote something on the ceiling and told Lennon to climb up and see what she wrote. When he did and saw the word *yes* written there, he said a bond was immediately formed between the two. Ono would become his second wife. That day in November was the ninth.

John Lennon believed so strongly that the number 9 had a direct influence on his life that he wrote songs dealing with the number over the years. Lennon and McCartney teamed up to write the song "One After 909" early in their career, and John wrote "#9 Dream" and "Revolution 9." The latter song ends with John saying "number 9" over and over until the song fades to silence.

Believe what you will, but it seems that the number 9 was certainly an integral part of John Lennon's life. But I will have to leave the meaning and importance of this to those who know more about numerology than I do. Even if we toss out the possible supernatural cause of the number 9 appearing so often throughout Lennon's life, it is certainly an odd coincidence that John should be born on the ninth day of the month and die on the eighth of the month. That is, the eighth day in the United States; it was the ninth of December in the town of his birth in Britain.

10

PRINCE, TUPAC AND NAYA RIVERA

P rince Rogers Nelson, more commonly known as Prince, is another star who is thought of primarily as a singer-songwriter. But Prince appeared in a number of films in the 1980s and '90s, one of which, *Purple Rain*, earned him the Academy Award for Best Original Song Score. Prince went on to become a film director, producer and star, but his claim to fame came from his music, and that is the main source of his fan base. And Prince's fans were and are some of the most devoted in music history.

Prince died at the age of fifty-seven from a fentanyl overdose on April 21, 2016, and as we have seen with other celebrities, he seems to have had the gift of prophecy, or so his sister and devoted fans believe. During a 2017 interview on the British talk show *Lorraine*, Tyka Nelson spoke of a strange telephone call she had with her brother in 2013, a full three years before he overdosed. Nelson said she received a call from an unknown number and was surprised to hear her brother when she answered. She said he acted weird, trying to get her to verify that it was actually her, until she told him that she remembered his voice after years of not speaking and said she knew it was her brother.

Tyka Nelson went on to say that her brother was acting very strange and that he seemed to be predicting his death. "We were just walking and talking and he said, 'I think I've done everything I've come to do.'" Nelson said that after she hung up the phone, she began looking to buy jewelry for her brother's funeral and telling their relatives that his days were numbered. "So, it took an actual three years from the time I got the call at McDonald's…

when I got the call that he had passed. I knew immediately what they meant because I was just kind of waiting for that day." Tyka Nelson said that from the moment she hung up the phone after talking to Prince, she knew her brother had called to tell her he was going to die. She said that she believes it is the family's Native American heritage that made her and her brother capable of such things as premonitions.

It wasn't only Prince's family that was made aware of the singer's impending doom. As many believe, the star's fans were told by Prince himself. Fans began to wonder about the singer's state of mind following his release from the hospital after having suffered severe flu symptoms. Prince, wanting to make sure his fans knew that he was alive and well, hosted a party at his estate a couple of days later. Although he didn't perform, he did get up on stage and told those gathered, "Wait a few days before you waste any prayers on me." Less than four days later, he was found dead in his elevator. One fan posted on Twitter, "Sounds like he knew he was dying."

Many of his fans say that he left a message in his track "Sometimes It Snows in April," which has the chorus, "Sometimes it snows in April, sometimes I feel so bad, sometimes I wish life was never ending and all good things, they say, never last." The song is about losing someone. As Prince died in the month of April, the coincidence is a glaring one. A fan on Twitter wrote, "It snowed in April and then he died. Prince predicted his own death. #restinpeace." It was also pointed out that in his song "Let's Go Crazy," there is the lyric, "Things are much harder than in the afterworld in this life / You're on your own and if de-elevator tries to bring you down go crazy (punch a higher floor.)" Prince was found overdosed in the elevator of his home. Many believe that this section of the song was meant as a warning to his followers. "Prince was found in an elevator and in 'Let's Go Crazy,' Prince says 'If the elevator tries to break you down' and it honestly gives me chills," tweeted a longtime fan.

Many of these things can be attributed to coincidence, but when added together they constitute what many believe to be proof that Prince knew his time was coming; maybe, as his sister Tyka believes, at least three years before his death. I will let my readers decide what they believe, but it seems that his sister and his devoted fans have already made up their minds.

TUPAC SHAKUR IS ANOTHER singer turned movie star who predicted his death. For those close to him, he made the prediction many times over the years. On September 7, 1996, Shakur left the MGM Grand in Las Vegas after watching a Mike Tyson fight and was sitting in the passenger seat of the BMW owned by Death Row Records founder Suge Knight. While they waited for a red light to change at the intersection of Flamingo Road and Koval Lane, a white Cadillac with California plates pulled up next to the BMW. Shots rang out from the Cadillac, and Tupac was hit four times. One bullet hit the rapper in the hand, another in his pelvis. He could have survived these wounds. But two bullets also entered Tupac's chest. He died at a hospital six days later at the age of twenty-five.

Tupac's fans were in a state of shock. Many blamed Knight, believing he had Tupac killed because the rapper was planning on leaving Death Row Records. Others blamed gang members whom Tupac had been in a fight with shortly before he was ambushed. Whatever the case, the up-and-coming actor was dead. Tupac had called the age of his death more than two years before his passing. In an interview on the Art of Dialogue YouTube channel, friend and fellow rapper Smooth B talked about a conversation he had with Tupac a couple of years earlier in which Tupac said: "I've already seen death. I know how I'm gonna go out." Smooth B went on to tell how he told Tupac that he believed he would be a good dad, but Tupac replied: "I ain't gonna be around long enough to have kids. I'm telling you I ain't gonna live past 25." Smooth B said he was floored when he heard the news about his friend's death. He said it was as if Tupac had predicted his death at that age, as though he really knew he was going to die at twenty-five.

This was not the only time Shakur told friends and family he wouldn't live past twenty-five. He told his mother on more than one occasion that he was caught up in a lifestyle he couldn't seem to get out of, no matter how hard he tried, and that it was going to kill him by the time he turned twenty-five. Other friends have said he told them the same thing, but many believed the rapper was just being dramatic. Two years before his death, Shakur was involved in another shooting. While Shakur was recovering from five gunshot wounds, journalist A.J. Benza interviewed the rapper and recalled him saying, "I'm going to die young. There is nothing that is going to stop it."

Many of Tupac's fans believe that he foretold his death in songs. In his hit "If I Die 2night," he raps, "I hope they bury me and send me to my rest / Headlines readn' murdered me to death, my last breath." A song by Richie Rich, "Niggas Done Changed," features Tupac. He sings the line, "I been shot and murdered, can tell you how it happened word for word / But best believe that niggas gon' get what they deserve." If the lyrics in these songs weren't enough to convince his fans that he predicted how he would die,

Tupac Shakur was killed at this intersection in Las Vegas, Nevada.

the release of his final video, recorded just a month before his murder and released only three days after his death, provides the most eerie possible proof. The video for "I Ain't Mad at Cha" shows Tupac getting shot several times after leaving an event. In the video, Tupac dies and arrives in heaven to see Billie Holiday, Jimi Hendrix, Miles Davis and Louis Armstrong jamming together and having fun. The similarities between this video and his actual murder are chilling.

Although Tupac died in 1996, it seems that he was not ready to move on to the afterlife or to jam with other famous musicians. His ghost has been seen often at the corner of Koval and Flamingo, leaning against the light pole at the spot where he was gunned down. His spirit has also been seen on the balcony of what used to be Suge Knight's Las Vegas home and in the room where he was staying at the Luxor Hotel when he was murdered. Tupac has also been seen at recording studios in New York and Los Angeles.

After Shakur's death, fans began to form all sorts of conspiracies about his death. One theory holds that rapper Biggie Smalls ordered Tupac's death to end the East Coast / West Coast rapper war and that is also why Smalls was killed shortly after Tupac's murder—as revenge. Another theory has Tupac in the witness protection program and that he is still testifying against criminals such as Knight. Some folks believe that Shakur faked his death and is living in Cuba with his aunt and has become a leader in the New Black Panther Party. Today, many fans believe that Shakur has returned to music and that the holographic images projected onto the stage are in fact Tupac Shakur himself. True fans never give up hope of seeing their idols again, and they do so with unrealistic expectations. But if it gives them comfort, who are we to disagree with them?

UNLIKE PRINCE AND TUPAC Shakur—singers who became actors—Nya Rivera began on the screen in the television show *Glee* and, because of her incredible voice, transitioned into a successful music career. Rivera first appeared in commercials after she did work as a child model. She landed her first role at the age of four in the CBS sitcom *The Royal Family*. Her big break came when she landed the role of Santana Lopez on the Fox television show *Glee*. She received critical acclaim for her portrayal of a lesbian cheerleader and won Screen Actors Guild (SAG) and American Latino Media Arts (ALMA) Awards and was nominated with the entire cast for two Grammy Awards and a Brit Award. From there, Rivera starred in a few movies and launched her music career when she signed with Columbia Records in 2011. Naya Rivera's star was on the rise, and it seemed that nothing could stop her.

Fate has a way of interfering when we least expect or want it to, and this seems to be the case with Rivera. On July 8, 2020, Rivera, needing a break and wanting to spend time with her four-year-old son, drove from their home in Santa Clarita, California, to Lake Piru a short distance away. Once at the lake, Rivera rented a pontoon boat and set off for an afternoon of swimming and floating in the clear waters. This was the last time Rivera was seen alive. Her fans now believe that Rivera, by way of a tweet, was trying to tell them that she was going to die, even if her "prediction" was thin at best.

When Naya Rivera and her son, Josey, failed to return to the dock with their rented boat at the scheduled time of 4:00 p.m., a search party was sent to look for them. When the boat was spotted, they saw that Rivera's son was sound asleep, but there was no sign of his mother. After a full day of searching for Rivera and not finding her, the search was called off and a recovery was instituted. It was believed that Naya was most likely dead. Her body was found on July 13, and the coroner gave accidental drowning as the official cause of death. Many of her fans, however, don't believe it was an accident.

Naya Rivera is buried near Carrie Fisher.

Some fans believe that a post on Twitter five days before Naya's drowning was her premonition that she was going to be killed. The tweet showed a picture of her cuddling with her son and the words "Just the two of us" displayed below it. She also posted a tweet that read: "Make the most of today and every day you are given. Tomorrow is not promised." Some people believe that the tweet of Naya and her son was a reference to a song by rapper Eminem about a mother being killed by the father of their son. In the song, "Just the Two of Us," the father drowns the woman. Some fans think that Naya's ex-husband killed her while their son was asleep on the boat. The song's lyrics include, "Dada made a nice bed for mommy at the bottom of the lake." This is a spooky coincidence to be sure, but when compared to other premonitions from stars, it falls short. This seems to be a case of fans trying to make sense of a star's death.

Death is always a hard thing to comprehend, but when it happens to someone we have made into an idol and symbol in our lives, it becomes that much harder. For Naya Rivera's fans to equate the words, "just the two of us," to the Eminem song is understandable, but it is highly more likely that if Rivera was referencing a song at all it was probably the song of the same name sung by Grover Washington Jr. that she was referencing. Accident or murder, the death of Naya Rivera left a hole not only in the hearts of her family, but also in the millions of folks that still call themselves her fans.

PART III

GHOSTS AND LEGENDS

11

RUDOLPH VALENTINO AND FALCON LAIR

Rudolph Valentino passed away in 1926, but even today he is considered the consummate Latin lover, a heartthrob second to none and the forerunner of every male sex symbol who followed. Many women at the time swooned at the mention of Valentino's name, and when he died, it is said that hundreds of ladies committed suicide rather than live in a world without him. Even as a twice-married man, Valentino was sought after by female fans who thought they could lure him away from his wife and become the new Mrs. Valentino. He was what is now known as pansexual; he fell in love not only with his two wives but also with his protégé, Ramon Novarro. It seems that Rudolph Valentino is still at his old haunts after all these years. Perhaps he isn't ready to give up his love for Novarro. Or maybe, having died at the young age of thirty-one, Valentino isn't ready to give up the limelight.

Rodolfo Alfonso Raffaello Pierre Filiberto Guglielmi di Valentina d'Antonguella was born in 1895 in Castellanetta, Italy. When Rodolfo was eleven years old, his father passed away from malaria, and the young boy was basically forced to fend for himself. His father, a former military officer, had enrolled his son in military school, but he was rejected from service, reportedly for being too frail. Taking on odd jobs to survive, in 1912, Rodolfo moved to Paris to look for work. Unable to find a suitable job and having to beg on the streets, Rodolfo made his way to New York City in 1913. Once in the Big Apple, he worked as a gardener, a dishwasher, a dance partner and an uncredited actor in a few films.

It was this view that originally persuaded Rudolph Valentino to purchase the home that would become known as Falcon Lair.

While Rodolfo was working at a nightclub, Maxim's, he was introduced to high society and hired by Chilean heiress Blanca de Saulles to work as her gardener. While there, Rodolfo was caught up in her nasty divorce. And Rodolfo testified for her, John de Saulles had him arrested for ambiguous "vice'" charges. Rodolfo was forced to flee the state to avoid scandal. In 1917, Blanca killed her husband. After brief stays in Utah and San Francisco, Rodolfo Guglielmi set his sights on Hollywood.

By 1918, Rodolfo had settled in Los Angeles and focused on acting as his career. Needing a simpler name that was easier to pronounce, he settled on the stage name Rudolph Valentino. Valentino had to settle for small roles but knew it was the only way to get noticed in Hollywood. In 1919, he married actress Jean Acker. She was reportedly a lesbian, and many people think the marriage was an effort on Valentino's part to further his career. It was reported that Acker locked Valentino out of their hotel room on their wedding night. The unhappy couple divorced in 1922, shortly after Valentino received his first starring role in a film.

In *The Four Horsemen of the Apocalypse*, Valentino's first scene has him dancing a tango with Beatrice Dominguez. This one scene solidified him as a star. His popularity grew rapidly, and studio press agents were able to capitalize on it. More roles came pouring in for the "Great Lover" of the 1920s. Valentino was cast in a series of romantic dramas, including *The Sheik* (1921) and *Blood and Sand* (1922). Not all of Valentino's films were successful, as *Monsieur Beaucaire* (1924) and *A Sainted Devil* (1924) can attest.

Valentino's appearances in these latter films may have been at the hands of his second wife, Natacha Rambova, whose real name was Winifred Shaughnessy. Rambova, a set designer, artistic director, screenwriter, producer and, it is said, lesbian lover of bisexual actress Alla Nazimova, was seen as a controlling woman who seemed to want Valentino under her thumb. While his divorce from Acker was not yet finalized, Valentino married Rambova. The marriage was annulled, and he was charged with bigamy. After paying a fine and waiting the required time, the two were remarried in 1923. It was thought that Rambova picked Valentino's roles for him. She chose parts that she said were more suited to his personality but made him seem more effeminate. She demanded to be on the set during filming and interfered. It wasn't long before the studio banned her from the set altogether. By the following year, an unhappy Valentino had divorced Rambova and went back to making the films he was known for.

Rudolph Valentino always struggled to gain the acceptance of male viewers; many men considered him unmanly. His sexually ambiguous good looks had men questioning his masculinity, with one columnist claiming in an op-ed titled "Pink Powder Puffs" that Valentino was responsible for the United States sinking into "degradation and effeminacy." In response to the article, Valentino wrote, "You slur my Italian ancestry; you ridicule upon my Italian name; you cast doubt upon my manhood." Even with all of the slurs brought by male moviegoers and the media, Valentino's box office success, especially with female audiences, didn't suffer in the least.

After his divorce from Rambova, Valentino starred in the movie *The Eagle* (1925), which once again cast him in the type of role that had made him famous in the first place. After this film, he starred in a sequel of sorts to his earlier hit *The Sheik*. *The Son of the Sheik* was arguably Valentino's most popular film, earning him praise for his performance. If he wasn't already known as America's heartthrob, this film solidified this status. Valentino was back. Unfortunately, he wouldn't live to make another film.

On August 15, 1926, while on a promotional tour for his new film, Valentino became ill and was rushed to New York Polyclinic Hospital, where he was diagnosed with gastric ulcers and appendicitis. He was taken to surgery. Doctors later said that everything had gone as planned, but shortly after being removed from a recovery room, the actor developed peritonitis, an inflammation of the abdomen and abdominal organs. Three days after surgery, doctors were optimistic about Valentino's recovery. But by August 21, his condition had declined. He had developed pleuritis, a condition in which the membranes around the lungs and chest cavity swell. Doctors knew that the chance of recovery was slim. On August 23, Valentino regained consciousness, spoke to his doctors about his future, slipped into a coma and died. He was thirty-one years old.

It is estimated that one hundred thousand people attended Valentino's funeral. A few unruly fans smashed windows trying to get in, and many despondent fans committed suicide. It took over one hundred officers of the New York Police Department and Police Reserve to restore order. A second, smaller funeral was held in Hollywood, as people gathered to lay Valentino to rest in Hollywood Memorial Park. Rudolph Valentino died at the height of his career but so far has refused to move on to the other side of the veil. He is still seen at his old home in Beverly Hills; in a hotel in Santa Maria, California; and in a hotel turned apartments in Hollywood.

As mentioned earlier, Natacha Rambova was considered a controlling woman and, while married to Rudolph Valentino, wanted all the perks that came with the marriage. This meant moving from their cozy home in the Whitley Heights area of Hollywood to a sprawling estate in the elite and posh Benedict Canyon section of the Hollywood Hills. For his part, Valentino wanted the privacy the house afforded him. To satisfy them both, they purchased an eight-acre, eleven-bedroom, Spanish-style mountainside villa for $175,000 in 1925. They named it Falcon Lair, in honor of the movie they were planning on making together, *The Hooded Falcon*.

Rambova never lived in the estate, as the couple divorced before she could move in. But Valentino fell in love with the villa from the moment he moved in. He rode his horses on the sprawling property and used trails to visit his famous neighbors. He entertained guests with lavish parties and galas that were the envy of Hollywood. But most of all, Valentino loved the seclusion and privacy. Unfortunately, he didn't enjoy his villa for long, and after his sudden death in 1926, the estate was sold to New York diamond broker Jules Howard. He didn't move in but rented the main house to silent-film star Harry Carey. The villa was sold a few times over the years to art dealer Juan Romero, Doris Duke and actress Ann Harding, to name a few. Of the many folks who have lived in and owned Falcon Lair, most if not all told stories of spirits residing there. As far back as 1928, a reporter wrote an article about her paranormal experience in the home.

Reporter Ruth Biery was assigned by *Motion Picture Magazine* to spend the night in Rudolph Valentino's bedroom and write a story about the recently

Valentino loved the horse trails surrounding his home and used them to visit his neighbors.

deceased actor and the reports of his spirit coming back from the grave. The story she wrote, "I Slept in Valentino's Haunted House" (*Motion Picture Magazine*, volume 34, number 4, November 1928), makes it clear that Falcon Lair was haunted, maybe even before Valentino moved in. An excerpt from her story states that early in the evening, as she was writing, she heard shuffling footsteps coming up the stairs. As she paused, "pen raised," she saw the door open. Thinking it was her friends, Biery called out to them but got no response. After calling out again, she heard the footsteps retreat down the stairs, and she went back to writing. A few moments later, she heard her friends coming up the stairs, and when they entered the room, she asked why they hadn't answered her the first time they came up. Surprised, her friends told Biery that they hadn't come up until that moment.

The article also recounted how Biery had been awakened toward morning, "feeling as though someone had entered the room above me." She went on to write, "On the stairway was a shadow. I rose, approached. It disappeared. I sat down again. Once more the shadow appeared. I rose and approached this shadow. Was I insane or did it retreat up the stairs before me? I turned, picked up my cot, departed." As Biery was leaving, she ran into the caretaker, who asked, "Did you see anything?" She responded, "N-n-no," and left Falcon Lair, never to return.

Jules Howard owned the house but, as stated earlier, never lived there. His brother Alberto, however, moved into the guesthouse as caretaker while the main house was rented to various tenants. While caretaker, and before any renters moved into Falcon Lair's mansion, Alberto began seeing strange and eerie lights flashing inside the house and saw "ghost-like figures" moving about in the dead of night (*Los Angeles Times*, 1930). Alberto also said that folks living in the main house would continually ask him if the place was haunted. He said that he tried to reassure them that it wasn't; he also said that he knew they didn't believe him.

Harry Carey moved into Falcon Lair with his wife and two kids in 1930, over the objection of many friends who said the house was haunted. Carey said, "The stables were too good to pass up, you know I still have my horse, so, we moved in anyway." Carey may have regretted his decision almost immediately. On the first few nights, the entire family was kept awake by strange tapping noises. Carey once quipped, "Africa was wild, but our first several nights in the house were wilder."

Looking for mundane causes of the tapping sounds, Carey inspected the house and found a few possible sources. But despite this, Carey said: "Nevertheless, there is something strange and spooky about the place. In

Seclusion from the prying eyes of his fans gave comfort to Valentino.

spite of all we found out. When our lease expires, we're going back to the wide-open spaces of the ranch" (*Los Angeles Times*, 1930). Carey also said that he found out the caretaker of the property held séances in a room in the basement of the main house.

In 1946, Falcon Lair was purchased by Mrs. Gerald "Gypsy" Buys. Buys was extremely rich. It was rumored that she had a drawer filled with jewels labeled for wearing for each day of the week. Not only was Buys wealthy, she was also a Valentino fanatic. Two years after buying the estate, she held a séance in the main house on what would have been the star's fifty-third birthday. The *Los Angeles Times* reported what happened during the séance. "The psychics, seated in a circle, called on Valentino to make his presence known. He responded...with various manifestations felt mostly within the spiritualists themselves. One saw him appear at the window, while others... received spoken messages from the screen lover" (*Los Angeles Times*, 1948)

Valentino's second wife, Rambova, maintained until her death in 1966 that she was in contact with her deceased ex-husband. She claimed that Valentino refused to believe he was dead, no matter how hard or how often she tried to convince him otherwise. This is why, according to Rambova, Valentino wouldn't leave his beloved Falcon Lair. Rambova said that he would "live" at the estate as if he was still among the living, walking the

Privacy was always on Valentino's mind, as this high gate can attest.

hallways, sleeping in his room, saddling his horses in the stables and riding on the trails he always loved. She always maintained that Falcon Lair was indeed haunted but that Valentino was unaware of the living persons who surrounded him.

The estate was across the street from the Sharon Tate murder house. One has to drive up Cielo Road to get to Falcon Lair. In the years following owner Doris Duke's death, the mansion sat vacant or otherwise fell into disrepair. Folks using maps of stars' homes or one of the many maps of Hollywood murder sites saw strange lights and figures moving within the main house, even though no one was living there or elsewhere on the premises. Common experiences of visitors include hearing the sounds of a horse clopping by with a quiet urging from an unseen rider and hearing the sounds of a man talking when no one can be seen.

While Valentino likes to stay around his beloved Falcon Lair and the privacy it allows him, his spirit has been seen at other places he frequented while alive. One of these is the Santa Maria Inn in Central California. Valentino loved traveling up the coast and to the city of Santa Maria. Whenever he was in the city, the Santa Maria Inn was his place to stay, and he always stayed in the same room, 221. Valentino is known to knock on the door when guests are staying in "his" room and has been felt sitting on the bed while folks are trying to sleep. At other times, guests will come into the room to see an indent in the bed, as if someone is lying in it. It seems that Valentino still likes to take his trips up the coast for a pleasant night's stay at his favorite hotel.

Valentino was entombed in the Cathedral Mausoleum at Hollywood Forever Cemetery, which is adjacent to the back wall of Paramount Studios. Many of the folks working at the studio have reported seeing Valentino visiting Paramount, usually dressed in his "Sheik" costume from the movie of the same name. The mausoleum appears not to be haunted by the actor but by a woman simply known as the "Lady in Black." She brings a single red rose to Valentino's crypt on the anniversary of his death. The spirit is thought to be the ghost of Ditra Flame, who in life showed up every year with a rose for the actor. After Flame passed away in 1984, the Lady in Black began to appear and has come every year since to leave a spectral rose, which vanishes shortly after the spirit departs.

Other places where Rudolph Valentino's spirit has been seen include the Knickerbocker Hotel (now a low-income apartment building); a beach house in Oxnard; and an apartment complex, Valentino Place, that was once a speakeasy where Valentino used to hang out. The house where Valentino and Rambova lived in Whitley Heights, referred to as Villa Valentino, was

All that remains of the great Falcon Lair is the guesthouse, some of the gardens and a few trails.

torn down years ago to make way for the Hollywood Freeway. The home was well known to be haunted by the actor. Even today, people report strange things at the site where the house once stood. Even Valentino's beloved Great Dane, Kabar, is said to sometimes lick the hands of folks who come to visit the dog's grave in the Los Angeles Pet Memorial Park in Calabasas.

The main house at Falcon Lair was torn down in 1996, and the entire estate was sold in 2021, with plans to build a thirty-thousand-plus-square-foot, modern Mediterranean mansion replete with huge patios, gardens, a pool and a wine-tasting room. One has to wonder if Falcon Lair is still haunted by its former owner. If so, how does he feel about this huge new structure at his once peaceful mountaintop estate? If the new owners decide that the horse trails are no longer needed, Rudolph Valentino might decide that it is time to give notice to those living nearby and make his displeasure known. Of course, if he approves of the new digs, the current owners may find themselves sharing their home with a happy Latin lover to help entertain guests they invite over.

12

THE STRANGE DEATH
AND CURSE OF THE HOT TODDY

Few people today have heard of actress Thelma Todd. As she passed away in 1935, it isn't hard to understand why folks might not be familiar with this incredible and beautiful talent. For those who know who the "Hot Toddy" was, they realize that her untimely death at the height of her career is still couched in mystery, innuendo and mob affiliations that darken her legacy to this day. What many of her present-day admirers may not know is that Thelma Todd might still be among the shadows of the living and might have put a curse on the "*Mary Celeste* of the Pacific."

Thelma Todd got her start in films in a roundabout way. After winning the Lawrence City Beauty Pageant, she was sent to Boston to represent the city in the Miss Massachusetts Pageant. There was abundant media attention and interviews with newspapers and magazines, and Todd's beauty and striking blonde hair caught the attention of Paramount Pictures executive Jesse Lansky. He immediately entered Todd into his new talent school, which was meant to foster prospective actors for the studio. On entering the school, Todd's immense talent all but guaranteed her a Hollywood career. The school was in New York City, so Todd and her mother moved there while Todd learned the ins and outs of performing on camera.

It wasn't long before Thelma Todd was given her first movie role with Paramount Pictures. Her debut film, *Fascinating Youth*, showcased her talent, and despite it being a minor role, the powers that be saw Todd's potential, and she was offered her first contract. The agreement was for just one year, but it included a wage of seventy-five dollars a week. Todd, having come

Thelma Todd more than deserved her star on the Hollywood Walk of Fame.

from a small town, never dreamed of making such a large sum of money. With the contract signed, Todd was immediately cast in her first feature film, *Popular Sin*, to be filmed in New York. Thelma's father had passed away before she graduated from school, and her mother, heartbroken by the loss of her husband, leaned on Thelma for emotional support. After the film wrapped up, Thelma, with her mother in tow, headed out west to Hollywood, where Thelma Todd would become known as the "Hot Toddy."

Paramount Studios set a fast-paced, demanding schedule for Thelma, with five films in her first year in Hollywood alone. The studio raised her weekly pay from $75 a week to $250, but with the stipulation that her weight stay below 120 pounds. When talking pictures arrived on the scene, many actresses fell short in adapting to the new medium. Thelma's first "talkie," *Seven Footprints of Satan*, was so successful that Paramount raised her salary to $300 a week and began promoting her as its new starlet. As Todd's fame grew, so did her reputation as Hollywood's newest party girl. Almost every night, Todd could be seen in the nightclubs, partying into the morning hours with

Hollywood actors, directors and producers. Despite the late-night activities, Thelma Todd became known as someone who could be counted on to never be late or absent from the set. She certainly stood out in Tinseltown for this alone. It was the party-girl persona that brought Thelma into contact with her first and only husband, known gigolo and mobster Pasquale "Pat" DiCicco. Thelma's interest in DiCicco may have been more about jealousy and her love of another man rather than love for her new husband.

In June 1931, Thelma was loaned out to United Artists to star opposite Chester Morris in director Roland West's film *Corsair*. West tried to get Todd to change her name for the film. He wanted to change her image, from that of a comedienne to that of a dramatic actress. West told everyone on set to call her Alison Loyd. Thelma opposed the name change, but after production began, Thelma found herself falling in love with West. This, together with her desire to be seen as a dramatic actress, caused Thelma to warm up to the idea of changing her screen name. *Corsair* is the only film in which Thelma appears with this name. As filming progressed, Thelma's love for West grew, and she fell hopelessly in love with the man. Thelma urged West to divorce his wife, silent-screen star Jewel Carmen, so that the two could be together. West, unwilling to leave his wife but still fond of Thelma, sailed to Mexico after the film wrapped on his private yacht, *MV Joyita*, to scout locations for his next film. He took Todd along for company. Roland West always said that their relationship was never romantic, however much Thelma might have wanted it to be. He said that he thought of her as a younger sister. Whether this was true or not will always be a matter of speculation. Thelma was devastated by his attitude toward her, and to ease her pain, she went out every night with her friend Lina Basquette, the ex-wife of Sam Warner. It was on one of these nights that she met the man she would marry and who would be a suspect in her murder just four years later.

DiCicco was known in Hollywood as a man who dated starlets in order to gain recognition and wealth; Thelma, it seems, didn't care. West's rejection was never far from her mind, and she may have looked to DiCicco to make West jealous in the hopes that he would change his mind and come for her. When Thelma was out on the town, she always made sure to be seen with DiCicco and went out of her way to go to places she knew West frequented. Her scheme didn't work, and with no other options and with at least some affection for DiCicco, she married him in 1932.

It didn't take long for DiCicco's true nature to come out, and the couple began to quarrel, with DiCicco yelling at and threatening Todd. It got to the point that neighbors began to threaten the couple with calling the police. But

Thelma loved her sidewalk café as well as her partner, Roland West.

things escalated, and DiCicco began to beat Thelma. He went so far as to run their car off the road, giving Todd a concussion and a broken shoulder. While in the hospital, Todd made the decision to divorce DiCicco as soon as possible. The couple's marriage ended in February 1934. By that time, Thelma Todd had been reunited with Roland West. That is, they had gone into business together.

Thelma knew that as she grew older, roles would dwindle and younger women would begin to replace her. To ensure a steady income in retirement, she approached West with the offer of a partnership. Thelma proposed that they open an upscale café to cater to the rich and famous and to use her star power and name to draw in customers. She hoped to use West's money to fund the venture. West agreed, and Thelma Todd's Sidewalk Café was soon up and running. Situated on Pacific Coast Highway directly across from the beach in Pacific Palisades, the café was an instant success. The restaurant had two levels, a casual, upscale café on the lower level and a reservations-only fine-dining room on the second floor. The first floor was almost always filled to capacity with tourists hoping to catch a glimpse of Thelma Todd. The upper floor, named Joya's Room, hosted Hollywood's elite along with the rich and famous from all over.

The location of the café couldn't have been better, as Roland West lived on the hill directly behind the café. It was a bit of a walk up steep stairs but close enough for easy access to the restaurant. The building itself had three levels, and Thelma moved into the apartments on the top floor. Roland and Thelma were together at the cafe every night. West's wife, Jewel, had been in recovery from a nervous breakdown, and West took it upon himself to look after and care for Thelma as well. They were private about their lives, and everyone knew that they had separate sleeping quarters, but they also knew that Thelma was never seen dating another man while she was with West. Thelma still went out unaccompanied almost every night to clubs, as she did on the last night anyone saw her alive.

After attending a party for her good friend Stanley Lupino at the Trocadero nightclub on Sunset Boulevard, Thelma was driven home and dropped off on Pacific Coast Highway near Thelma Todd's Sidewalk Café. After finding the doors locked and her keys missing, Thelma walked up the steep stairs to the garage, where she kept her prized Lincoln Phaeton. She climbed into the car to stay warm and fell asleep. Her body was found two days later, on Monday morning. Speculation, mystery and rumors about her death quickly spread and have continued to this day.

Rumors about the Hot Toddy's death began almost from the moment her body was found. Speculation that she was killed by Charles "Lucky" Luciano was one of the more popular theories. No one is sure how the myth came to be, but the story has it that Luciano came out to California. During a heated discussion while on the dance floor with Thelma, who refused to give over the café for Luciano's gambling interests, he threatened to kill her. The main problem with this theory is that Luciano never visited Thelma's café—or California, for that matter. Other theories have DiCicco killing his estranged wife; Roland West's wife, Jewel, killing Todd after finding out about the supposed affair; and West himself killing

The Trocadero Nightclub on Sunset Boulevard, where Todd spent her last evening out.

Todd to gain full control of the successful café. There was even a story that the police instituted a massive cover-up to keep the guilty party from being caught. Despite all the rumors and innuendo regarding the demise of Thelma Todd, it boils down to a simple case of accidental exhaust poisoning. Todd started the engine in a closed garage so that she could keep the heat running on a cold December night.

It may be the way Thelma died that keeps her on this mortal plane with unfinished business. Or she may remain among the living because of the rumors surrounding her death and her hope to clear her name over connections with the mob. Perhaps it is her love for Roland West that keeps her in the place they created together. Whatever the reason, it has become clear over the years that Thelma Todd remains in the café she came to call home.

After West divorced Jewel Carmen in 1938, he married actress and singer Lola Lane. He left the café to her after his death, but she didn't do much with the classic building on the coast. When she passed away in 1981, the building became a TV studio for Christian Paulist Productions. People working and acting at the studio claimed to see Thelma walking through the old café. She is most often seen coming down the stairs, making her way to the outside courtyard, where she stands, seemingly confused, before she glides toward

Pacific Coast Highway and vanishes. At other times, she wanders through what was once the lower café. She sometimes stops, seeming to pause at a table, before moving on and pausing again, as if she is making her rounds for the tourists dining at her establishment.

Upstairs, in what used to be the formal dining area, Joya's Room, Thelma has been seen doing the same thing as in the lower section of the café. When she is spotted upstairs, however, she is usually dressed in an evening gown. Though her appearance is almost translucent, one can tell that she is dressed to impress her Hollywood friends. She has also been seen in what were once her private apartments on the third floor. Here, she is seen not going about the business of entertaining but simply relaxing. People who have seen Thelma Todd in her old home claim that she simply paces. They say it looks as if she is waiting for something. When glimpsed here, she is wearing casual clothes from the 1930s. She was once seen wearing what appeared to be a nightgown and robe. It would seem that Thelma is just as comfortable in her sidewalk café in death as she was while alive.

Another area where paranormal activity is found relating to Thelma Todd is, of course, the garage where she was found dead. Over the years, visitors going to the garage have reported walking up to the door and hearing the sound of a car running. This happens even though the door is open and no car is visible. Residents living at the home today have had the same experience. Reports have come from them of the sound of a car idling in the garage at all hours of the day and night. It seems to be much more frequent around the hours of 3:00 and 4:00 a.m., the same time that Thelma would have been there trying to stay warm. Other reports from the garage mention the smell of carbon monoxide, or exhaust fumes. People have said the smell is so overwhelming that it makes them sick and has even caused some to flee the area for fear of passing out. The fumes grow even though there is no sound of an engine running or the presence of a car in the garage or nearby.

One of the main suspects in the possible murder of Thelma Todd was Roland West. People knew that Thelma was in love with West and that he shunned her affections. They knew that West was sometimes frustrated by her attentions. This, coupled with the belief that he wanted full control of the café, puts him firmly in the spotlight for her demise. West used to take Thelma with him to Catalina Island aboard the *MV Joyita*. They sailed to the island to relax. At other times, they took the boat out just to cruise the coast and unwind from the stress of business and filming. It was one of the things they both enjoyed, and they did it often. Because they were seen frequently aboard the yacht, it was believed that after Thelma got home from the

Trocadero on the fateful night, West took her on a relaxing night cruise and, once out at sea, murdered her. After the deed was done, he brought her ashore, placed her body in the Lincoln Phaeton and started the motor. The theory goes on to say that he then paid off the police and the coroner to cover up the actual cause of death and report the incident as an accidental death. There are many holes in this theory, but if true, it goes a long way to explaining a strange curse attached to the *MV Joyita* and its attaining the moniker the "*Mary Celeste* of the Pacific."

After Thelma passed away, Roland, saying that he could no longer sail on the yacht where he and Thelma spent so much time, sold the sixty-nine-foot *MV Joyita*. The yacht ended up in the Hawaiian Islands, where it was eventually turned into a U.S. Navy patrol boat. The *Joyita* sailed the islands for a year, looking for Japanese raiders during World War II, before it mysteriously beached itself on an uncharted reef. The navy refloated and repaired the vessel, again using it to patrol the islands. But strange things plagued the *Joyita* before the navy finally sold it in 1948. The new owners refurbished the *Joyita*, adding cork to the hull to make it more buoyant before installing heavy refrigeration equipment. The *Joyita* began its new life delivering refrigerated goods but again mysteriously ran aground in waters that were supposed to be clear, this time tearing its hull.

The *MV Joyita* was sold once again, this time to a university professor who leased the ship to a seasoned captain, Thomas "Dusty" Miller. Captain Miller delivered goods and equipment around the islands of the South Pacific and brought passengers looking for adventure on the high seas. On October 3, 1955, the *Joyita* was sailing from Apia, in Samoa, to the nearby Tokelau Islands, 270 miles away, when the ship, crew and passengers simply vanished. The Royal New Zealand Air Force searched an area of 100,000 square miles, but neither the ship nor any living soul was found. The yacht was eventually spotted drifting, partially submerged, on November 10 near the island of Vanua Levu, more than 600 miles from where it should have been. There was no one on board, the life rafts were missing and a doctor's bag was found on the deck containing a scalpel, stethoscope and four bloody bandages. The sextant and captain's logbook were missing, along with all navigational aids. In a mysterious move, someone had erected an awning over the flying bridge, and all of the lights had been left on. On the bridge, the radio showed that it had been tuned to the distress band, but it was discovered that a wire had shorted out, drastically reducing the range of the signal. This could account for the fact that no messages were received by the Coast Guard or by any other vessels.

This is the garage where Thelma Todd, trying to stay warm, died in the front seat of her prized Lincoln Phaeton.

Perhaps the strangest thing found onboard, and something no one to this day has been able to figure out, is why the starboard engine was completely covered with mattresses.

The fact that the *Joyita* was found partially sunk was very odd. When the ship sailed from Apia, its cargo hold was filled with empty fifty-five-gallon drums. This, coupled with all of the cork that had been installed throughout its hull, made the *MV Joyita* almost unsinkable. Why the crew and passengers would row away in the middle of the ocean in tiny rafts when the captain knew the ship would most likely stay afloat is also a mystery. The entire incident is another example of the strange events that surrounded the yacht following the death of Thelma Todd.

Once again, the *MV Joyita* was repaired and auctioned off, in 1956. In 1957, the yacht once again ran aground, this time carrying thirteen passengers. Repaired anew, the *Joyita* ran aground in 1959, then was repaired and sold once again. It wasn't long before the yacht again ran aground. But this time would be the last. The new owners decided not to refloat the ship, as the cost of refloating and repairing it wasn't worth it. The *Joyita* sat on its sandy perch, viewed as an odd tourist attraction, until 1970, when the sea and the weather finally reclaimed what was theirs.

When Thelma Todd was alive, the *Joyita* gave pleasure to its owner and friends and showed no sign that it was cursed. After Thelma's death, the *Joyita* brought nothing but mystery and death. Whether the stories are true that Thelma was killed at the hands of Roland West aboard the *Joyita* or that her restless spirit was the cause of all of the misfortune following the ship from owner to owner is up to my readers to decide. Perhaps, in Thelma's last gasp of life, she cursed Roland West, and that curse rebounded to the vessel. But considering what happened to the *MV Joyita*, it isn't hard to imagine that the boat truly was a ghost ship. This mystery has caused the yacht to become known as the *"Mary Celeste* of the Pacific," and it is listed as one of the top ten ghost ships in the world.

13

THE MYSTERY OF
THE HOUDINI ESTATE

Harry Houdini was known as a master of deception, the "King of Cuffs," "Master Magician" and "Master of Magic." His acts of daring escape and death-defying feats made him the highest-paid vaudeville act of all time and, in the early twentieth century, one of the highest-paid performers in the world. As an escape artist and magician, Houdini dazzled audiences with sleight of hand and physical prowess. But as the spiritual movement in America began to grow, Houdini used his knowledge of magic and his money to "out" the frauds within the movement. The desperate and heartbroken gladly gave over their money to charlatan mediums and soothsayers, who used their trickery to make folks think they were in contact with dead loved ones. But these tricksters were not safe from Houdini's wrath. It is possible that Harry Houdini's greatest illusion had nothing to do with magic, escape attempts or sleight of hand, but instead with an unintended misdirection about something as simple as where he lived.

Harry Houdini was born Erich Weisz on March 24, 1874, in Budapest, Hungary. His father, a rabbi, wanting to give his family a better life, immigrated to the United States and settled in the small town of Appleton, Wisconsin. Houdini later claimed that he was born there. When Erich was thirteen, he and his father moved to New York City, where his father took on odd jobs until the rest of the family joined them. It was in New York that Erich became interested in the art of the trapeze. After learning the ropes, he began performing in local circuses and vaudeville shows. Not seeing much success, Erich looked for other ways to perform. He always had an interest in magic, and he began learning sleight of hand and illusion. He started his own magic act in the same vaudeville shows he was familiar with, but he received only tepid reviews.

One of the things his fellow circus and vaudeville performers noticed about young Erich was his unusual strength and coordination. He became very good at picking locks and found that his strength was useful in getting out of tight spots. Erich was not a particularly large man, at five feet, six inches tall. This, coupled with his strength and agility, allowed him to escape from things that others could not. It wasn't long before Erich combined his two talents, magic and the art of escape, into one show. From Erich's first appearance using a combination of these skills, audiences raved at his abilities, and as word of mouth spread, his fame began to grow.

By 1894, Weisz's career had taken off. He was now a professional magician, and it was time for a new name to reflect his craft. As a child, Erich had the nickname "Ehrie," so it was a simple choice to change his first name to the more Americanized "Harry." While growing up, Erich admired the great French magician Jean-Eugène Robert-Houdin, so, in homage to this icon, Weisz chose the last name Houdini. Thus was born Harry Houdini, perhaps the greatest escape artist and magician history has ever known. Houdini later wrote a scathing book about Houdin and his lack of skill, *The Unmasking of Robert-Houdin*.

In the same year that Houdini the magician was born, Harry married fellow performer Wilhelmina Beatrice Rahner, or "Bess" to her husband and friends. Bess became Harry's lifelong stage assistant and performed under the name Beatrice Houdini. She gave advice and feedback to her husband on any new illusion or escape he came up with. No one else could give Harry advice, but he always listened to Bess. She truly was his partner in all things.

Beginning about 1900, Houdini's reputation began to spread around the globe, and he began performing for international audiences. Houdini escaped from ropes, handcuffs and shackles, and then he began to add milk cans, prison cells and even coffins to his act. With each device he escaped from, his fame grew. Houdini added ever-more daring feats to his repertoire, including an outdoor exhibition in which he had himself locked in a box and submerged underwater from a boat. The gathered crowd was in awe as he freed himself and climbed back on board. In another feat of derring-do, Houdini was put into a straightjacket, suspended upside down seventy-five feet above the audience and freed himself while the crowd watched.

In 1899, entertainment manager Martin Beck took notice of Houdini and began booking him with some of the best vaudeville shows in the world. Local police were recruited to lock Houdini into shackles and cuffs, tie him up and place him in prison cells and other places. This alone made the crowd believe that there was no way for the man to escape and added to the tension of the show. As the years and spectacles passed, Houdini became a huge sensation and the highest-paid American performer in history. But while amassing his wealth, Houdini didn't just spend his earnings on frivolous comforts. He was a man of honor, and after seeing what was going on in the spiritualist movement and the way people were bilked out of their money—many of them while mourning lost loved ones—he decided to use his fame and money to do something about it.

As president of the Society of American Magicians, Houdini was angry about the sheer number of fraudulent psychic mediums in America. He was upset not only that they were tricking people out of their money, but also that they were causing folks to distrust legitimate magicians and see them in a bad light. Houdini decided that the charlatans needed to be exposed to the public, and he began a vigorous campaign to do just that. One well-known instance of Houdini's work involved renowned psychic Mina Crandon, known as Margery. This ended Houdini's longtime friendship with Sir Arthur Conan Doyle. Doyle believed in Margery and the spiritualist movement so much that he could never forgive Houdini for ruining her reputation.

Even as Harry Houdini was fighting the frauds of the spiritualist movement, he and his wife, Bess, were studying it and making plans for their own experiment to find out if the spiritual realm was real and if there was indeed life after death. Harry and Bess, although not complete believers in spiritualism, figured that it couldn't hurt to find out. To this end, they made a pact with each other: the first one to die would, within a year of their death, make contact with the other. In this way, the answer would be revealed once and for all. Harry was the first to pass away, dying, fittingly, on Halloween night in 1926. Bess, true to their pact, held a séance the following year to make contact with her husband, but the experiment failed. Bess continued to try to reach her beloved husband every year until her own death, but with no luck. Bess Houdini eventually declared their experiment a failure in 1943. Although Bess never made contact with her husband, her attempts figure prominently in the mystery of a mansion in Hollywood that Houdini never owned but is nonetheless called the Houdini Estate.

When Harry Houdini began making films in 1916, Hollywood noticed. Eventually, he came out to Tinseltown to film, during which he stayed at the Alexandria Hotel in downtown Los Angeles. That is, until he met Ralph "Ralf" M. Walker. The two became friends, and Walker, who owned a large estate in the Laurel Canyon area of the Hollywood Hills, invited Harry and Bess to stay in his guesthouse while Harry was working on his films. The mansion where Walker resided, said to have been built in 1915, stood at 2398 (later 2400) Laurel Canyon Boulevard. The Mediterranean-style villa had three stories, eleven bedrooms, nine baths, a ballroom with a fifteen-foot stage, a huge patio, a pool and gardens, all on a very large plot of land. Besides the enormous main house, Walker built a four-bedroom guesthouse on the property across the street from the mansion, and it was here that Houdini stayed while in Hollywood. Here is where things get a bit mysterious.

Over the years, an urban legend has developed around the estate that Harry Houdini owned and built the mansion and lived there until his death from peritonitis in Detroit. We know this is not the case, as there are no records of Houdini ever owning a house, let alone an estate, in California. The rumor may have started sometime in the 1960s, after the estate burned to the ground in a 1959 Laurel Canyon fire and remained vacant for years

Although Houdini never owned the Houdini Estate, today, the property capitalizes on that reputation by displaying a statue of the magician just outside the gates.

afterward. It is rumored that Walker bequeathed Harry Houdini the estate after Walker died. But, as Walker died nine years after Houdini, this is not only unlikely but also a rather ignorant belief. Suffice it to say, Houdini never owned the property. He was most assuredly a frequent guest, even though some people say that he never set foot on the property.

The website Weird California (and its source, Creepyla.com) claims that there is no way Houdini ever stayed at or near the estate. As evidence for this, the website says the author of the Creepyla piece grew up in Laurel Canyon near the Houdini Estate some fifty years after Houdini died. Growing up, he never heard about Houdini living in the area from other residents, so he assumed Houdini must have never lived there. Weird California goes into more detail and research about why it doesn't believe Houdini was ever there. But the website uses false assumptions and myth to illustrate its point.

Weird California claims categorically that Houdini always stayed at the Alexandria Hotel when performing his act or filming a movie. It claims that this was because of how close the hotel was to the studios and that the studios would have most likely put him up in the posh hotel. But the website gives no sources for any of the claims, simply stating that the stories regarding Houdini and his time at the estate are "a good story, but what a load of garbage." There are, however, many historical testimonials regarding Houdini's presence at the home and photographs proving that, at the very least, Houdini was a frequent guest at the estate.

Today, the new owner of the rebuilt estate uses the property for weddings, concerts and other events. Even if you don't want to believe the estate's website, which states: "Houdini used the estate's pool to practice his amazing feats of escape and illusion until a short time before his death in 1926. The magic and mystery…still remain with the property where Houdini's wife, Bess gave a famous party for five hundred magicians and lived for years after her husband died," Houdini historian Patrick Cullion has come up with so much proof that it is hard to dismiss his findings.

Cullion, on his website houdinisghost.com, says that he had been looking for proof that Houdini had indeed visited the Laurel Canyon home of Walker and finally came across photos showing Harry Houdini enjoying the pool at the estate. (See the bibliography for a link to the photos.) He goes on to say: "There's no question that Houdini lived in Laurel Canyon for the better part of a year. The photo is from 1919, taken while Houdini was in Hollywood to make two pictures with Lasky-Famous players. The studio was located on Vine Street and took up a large area between Sunset Boulevard and Prospect (now Hollywood) Boulevard. A whole community of filmmakers lived around the studio. Houdini rented a guesthouse from Ralf M. Walker, a Los Angeles department store magnate."

Cullion also said that Bess Houdini moved back into the guesthouse after her husband's death and for the next few years would refer to her "home in Hollywood." After moving back to 2435 Laurel Canyon in 1934, she conducted a series of séances. When, in 1935, there was a magician's convention, Bess threw a cocktail party for five hundred magicians and their wives. The party was held in the gardens of the main estate. When Ralf Walker died in 1935, Bess moved out the following year, when the estate was sold. Cullion found a 1934 photo of a group of people at a lavish Hollywood Christmas party. In it, Bess Houdini; Harry's first partner, Dr. Jacob Hyman; and Ralf M. Walker and his wife are seated on the floor of the estate's ballroom. Also in the photo are many early Magic Castle members, along with Caryl Fleming, a Hollywood film director.

No, Harry Houdini never owned the estate that now bears his name, but it is certain that he visited it often and most likely lived there for a time. It is also now known that Bess lived there for some time after Harry's death. Those who contend with certainty that Houdini had no connection whatsoever with the estate seem, in a word, mistaken. The mystery of how this urban legend came to be is unknown. The same is true of the rumor that Houdini built and owned the Houdini Mansion. The mystery is deepened by the confusion over another mansion a short distance away on Laurel Canyon Boulevard. It is used as a recording studio and is sometimes mistaken for the Houdini Mansion. Confusion aside, one thing most folks know about the Houdini Estate is that it is a very haunted location.

According to the Houdini Estate, Harry, living across the street, would use tunnels constructed below Laurel Canyon Boulevard from the guesthouse to the gardens of the main house. (The estate claims that these tunnels are still there but are sealed off for safety reasons.) Houdini apparently used the tunnels to practice his escapes in the pool and in a water tank made especially for him. Houdini not only used the pool for his illusions; he also loved swimming and hanging out with his wife and friends around the pool and gardens of the estate. As Houdini loved Laurel Canyon and the home of his friend, it shouldn't come as a surprise that Harry would come back after death to continue to enjoy all that the estate has to offer.

In the years following the fire in Laurel Canyon and the destruction of the original mansion, people living in the area began to see a strange light on the grounds of the estate. Residents claim that the light slowly moves along the remaining walkways of the old garden as if out for a stroll in the cool evening air. Many of those witnessing this believe it is the ghost of Harry Houdini, who, it was known, liked to walk among the gardens in the evenings and early mornings. Harry also loved to walk through the hills behind the guesthouse. There have been reports of seeing a man dressed in 1920s clothing strolling among the trees in these hills, as if walking on long-forgotten trails. Many people have been surprised when the figure passes through bushes as if they weren't there before vanishing from sight.

The pool is another favorite of Harry Houdini now that the mansion has been rebuilt. It is said that people hosting events at the estate have actually seen Harry diving into the pool, headfirst, hands extended and together in a typical dive pose. They say that just before he enters the water, he vanishes. There is never any splash or sound, as if it never happened. The main house itself is said to have at least one spirit residing in it, although no one is sure who it might be. Many believe that it is not, in fact, Harry Houdini, as he never lived in the house but only visited. Some believe it might be the spirit of Ralf Walker. But, again, no one is sure.

The *National Enquirer* wrote a story about rapper Drake and how he was "scared away" from the Houdini Estate while filming a promotional video. The article, "Drake Hits the Breaks at Haunted Houdini House," reports the following:

> *Famed for his trademark cool-as-a-cucumber persona, Canadian-born crooner Drake suddenly turned terrified/chilled to the bone, even though it was hot as hell in L.A., while shooting a hush-hush TV promo at the allegedly haunted estate of legendary magician Harry Houdini!*
>
> *The "Hotline Bling" singer kept freaking that Houdini's haunt lies smack in the middle of creepy, winding Laurel Canyon, where L.A. lore famously claims ghosts, ghouls and witches have roamed the windswept hillsides for decades.*
>
> *Totally terrified, twitching at every creepy creak or chilly draft on his cheek, distraught Drizzy, saying he felt like he was burning in the "hotline to hell," finally performed his own magic, abruptly disappearing down the path back to his car at a, er…dead run.*

There is some speculation about the story, and the *Enquirer*'s reputation is not exactly stellar. But this article does show that the ghost stories attached to the estate have become common enough that a national publication would write about them.

Even though Creepyla.com gets it wrong about Houdini living or staying in Laurel Canyon, their story referenced earlier does put forth a possible explanation as to who the spirit at the old estate might be. The author of the piece states that while they were growing up near the Houdini Estate, a murder on the grounds took place and the murderer was sent to a mental institution. This story was confirmed by a longtime resident of the area, who said that the murderer's name was John F. (he couldn't recall the last name) and that John had killed his grandmother after she intervened in a fight between John, who was holding a knife, and John's grandfather. After years in an insane asylum, John was released, legally changed his name to Robin Hood and moved into the tunnels of the Houdini Estate. It seems that John may not have been sane at the time of his release, as he believed he actually was the Prince of Thieves and that Laurel Canyon was Sherwood Forest.

After moving into the caves, Robin Hood attempted to rape various women there after picking them up on Sunset Boulevard. Kids in the neighborhood tried to catch a glimpse of Robin, and whenever he was seen, the kids would swear he was a ghost. After a time, sightings of Robin Hood stopped, and people figured he had finally moved on. But then his body was found in the caves after a foul smell was reported. From the time Robin Hood's body was removed, folks in the area have reported seeing him near the caves and wandering Laurel Canyon.

Laurel Canyon isn't the only place Harry Houdini's spirit is known to haunt. It is widely believed that his spirit haunts the Le Parisien Theater in downtown Montreal, Canada. This venue is where many believe Houdini received the blow to his abdomen that eventually resulted in his death. Houdini had been performing at the venue, originally named the Princess Theatre, when, after a show, two McGill University students entered Houdini's dressing room. During their conversation, they said that they were suspicious of Houdini's abilities. Houdini told one of the students, Gordon Whitehead, that he could punch Houdini in the stomach to test his control of his own body. Without warning and without allowing Harry to prepare himself, Whitehead delivered four powerful blows to Houdini's abdomen. Because Houdini was unable to tighten his muscles, the punches ruptured his appendix, and this ultimately caused his death in a Detroit hospital.

Since Houdini's death, the Le Parisien Theater has had several reports of Houdini's spirit. Whenever he is seen, it is in full formal attire, replete with top hat and cape. Sometimes, Harry is seen sitting in the audience; at other times, he is on stage as if giving a show. During the venue's iteration as a multiscreen movie theater, guests marveled as Houdini was witnessed on an unseen stage going through his magic and escape routine. In 2002, a fire tore through the theater, destroying one auditorium and damaging six others.

Today, the building is for rent. One wonders if the history of its haunts will deter potential tenants from signing a lease.

Other places said to be haunted by Harry Houdini are, in Detroit, the site of the old Grace Central Hospital, now a professional building; the spot where the Garrick Theater once stood; and the site where Wm. R. Hamilton's Funeral Home once stood. This is where Houdini's body was prepared for burial. He is also supposedly seen in Greenwich Village in New York City. Author Tom Ogden, in his book *Haunted Greenwich Village* (Globe Pequot, 2012), suggests that Houdini haunts McSorely's Old Ale House. His theory claims that Houdini returns to his old watering hole in the form of a black phantom cat that is seen sitting in the window, then disappears. Niagara Falls is another spot where Houdini makes an appearance, this time in the Houdini Magical Hall of Fame. It is not known if Harry has returned since the museum closed for good in 1995.

Whether or not you believe that Harry Houdini haunts the estate that somehow bears his name—or anywhere else for that matter—he might have actually given his beloved wife her answer after his death, unfortunately without her realizing it. During the final public séance in 1936, which was broadcast on radio, Bess repeatedly begged her husband to bring a message. Not receiving one, she gave up trying with the words, "My last hope is gone. I do not believe Houdini can come back to me—or anyone....It is finished. Good night, Harry." At the exact moment she finished, a violent thunderstorm broke out, bringing with it a spectacular lightning show and a deluge of rain. The strangest thing about this particular storm was that it was localized only over the hotel where the séance was being held and spread out only a block on either side. It seems that Harry Houdini may have been saying goodnight to his wife in typical Houdini fashion.

14

THE MEDIEVAL TORTURE MUSEUM

In a town as old as Hollywood, it should come as no surprise that the buildings along Hollywood Boulevard change along with the times. What was once a drugstore might now be a gaudy gift shop catering to tourists, and what was once a grand movie palace might now be an industrial building stuffed with telecommunications equipment for a phone company. After all, what is Hollywood if not a make-believe world standing behind the façade of a thousand interchangeable movie sets. Into this ever-changing street front of musical chairs sits one of those buildings that have had many different uses over the years. Today, it may have its most unusual iteration of all: the Medieval Torture Museum.

This is perhaps one of the strangest museums you will visit, but also one of the most interesting. It is filled with devices illustrating man's inhumanity to man. Although we get to tour the rooms and faux dungeons with the comfort of knowing these torture tools are no longer used, we also feel, on some level, the pain the victims must have felt at the hands of the devices' creators. As weird as this museum may seem, it is a truly interesting and entertaining way to spend a few hours. As my wife says, the place is "creepy cool."

I had the pleasure of being shown around the building by the curator and general manager of the museum, Roberto Sanchez. He took me around not only the museum proper but also other, now abandoned areas of the building where, according to Robert, many ghostly tales have originated. The building itself is huge. There was once a venue next to the Torture Museum called the Max. According to Robert, it was some sort of weird selfie museum. I

Inside the Museum of Selfies.

was told that here folks still hear the sound of people shuffling around inside the now empty space, but when security goes to investigate, there is nobody inside and no signs of forced entry.

Another part of the building is a multistory office complex that, according to security personnel, cannot seem to keep its doors from shutting and locking on their own. Many of the guards say they have been called in the middle of the day to unlock an office door an employee left open when stepping out to get the mail or pick up a delivery, only to find the door closed and locked by an unseen hand. Most of these doors need a key to be locked, and after the guard lets the employee back into the office, the keys to the door are found on the desk, right where the worker left them. How the doors become locked is a mystery, as they need to be locked from the outside. One strange feature of this office section of the building is an entire floor that is simply bare drywall. The drywall is set up in no certain order, with no rhyme or reason, and it has never been explained why the floor has remained this way for so many years, instead of being converted to usable space.

Another area of the building was at one time a nightclub called the Day After. The club eventually shut down and became another selfie museum, simply and aptly named the Museum of Selfies. This actually wasn't a proper museum but rather a series of rooms with different props set up where folks could snap selfies of themselves amid unusual decor. Reports of strange things happening in this section of the building began almost immediately after the nightclub shut down in 2016. Folks heard footsteps on the old nightclub stage, even when no one was near the stage, let alone walking on it. Things would and do have a tendency to move around on their own. Many times, employees of the Museum of Selfies would open up in the morning and find that the sets had been completely rearranged overnight. Props had been moved from one room to another, sometimes completely across the museum. These situations occurred even though there was no sign of a break-in or that anyone had been in the museum overnight. No one is sure who the possible ghosts might be in these areas of the building, but none of the activity comes close to that at the Medieval Torture Museum in the basement of the building.

From the moment you walk through the doors of the Medieval Torture Museum, you feel that something is different about the place. It shouldn't be surprising, especially when you consider the museum itself has a collection of torture devices imported from Europe, most of which have actually been used for their intended purposes. A tool used to inflict pain and death can and will absorb the emotions it brings out in those being

This oven, shaped like a bull, is one of the more barbaric torture devices you will find in the Medieval Torture Museum.

tortured and then emit those feelings back on people nearby. This may be what is going on in the museum.

As you walk down the steps into the basement of the building and into the museum, the first room you come to includes a not-so-menacing copper bull. You notice a rope attached to the bull. When you pull the rope, which raises a panel on the side of the bull, a panel opens and you see the dummy of a human being roasting inside the copper bull, you realize the device is not as mundane as you had thought. This room is filled with stretching racks, flaying devices and whipping boards. Maybe it is the shock of seeing these devices for the first time, but some folks speak of having an immediate feeling of dread in this room, and some have to leave the museum before they even get started. One gentleman made it down to the bottom of the stairs, only to turn around. He passed out as soon as he got back to the top. When he regained consciousness, he said that as soon as his foot hit the museum floor, an overwhelming urge to flee came over him, and he knew something didn't want him there. He left without asking for a refund.

The second room on the tour, which Robert calls the Chair Room, is where you will find an electric chair, a spiked "interrogation" chair, a

The Chair Room has more to see than just diabolical torture seats.

pendulum and a few impaling spikes. Some exhibits graphically show how they worked. According to Robert, many guests who come into this room feel something brush past them. Thinking it is another museum patron, some turn to excuse themselves but find the room completely empty. Some have also claimed that as they turned to see who bumped them, they again felt something brush past, now in the opposite direction. Of all the rooms in the museum, the Chair Room has had the most people flee in terror, not asking for a refund and many refusing to even stop and explain why they are leaving in such a hurry. Many folks have also said that the chairs seem to give off an aura of bad energy. Still others say they feel as if the chairs are drawing away energy from them, causing a feeling of despair and hopelessness.

The Guillotine Room is supposed to stay warm. This room includes a simulation of a victim roasting on a spit over an open fire. The fire the museum uses is of course not real, but to achieve some semblance of reality, a faux fire is created with an attached heater, one designed to keep the room warm. The odd thing about this room is that even with the heater in full force, the room can become bone-chillingly cold. It has become so cold on occasions that guests have actually complained about the temperature.

Many times, an employee will head to the room to check the heater after a complaint, only to find the heater working and the room as cold as the guest claimed it to be. No cause has ever been found to explain the extreme cold in this heated room.

The Guillotine Room is also known to give folks an extreme feeling of unease. Many have said that the feeling comes over them the minute they set foot in the room and that it leaves them just as quickly when they leave. Many people believe that the ripsaw hanging on the wall behind the mannequin of an executioner may be the cause of this feeling. Many people who get near the ripsaw stop dead before getting too close. They say that the aura coming off this artifact is so strong that they physically can't get near it, that it becomes so uncomfortable as to actually repel them. Many flee this room to avoid the feeling of dread. But on leaving this room, they are headed to a place that many consider much worse.

This is an area called the Witches Torture Room. This small room is adjacent to the Sexual Torture Room. Together, these rooms make up by far the most haunted area of the museum. The Witches Torture Room contains masks that were used to cover a suspected witch's face in the hopes of keeping her from casting spells or enchantments. It also includes a series of branding irons used to mark a suspected witch for life—or death. In the

The Guillotine Room remains perpetually cold, even though it is meant to stay extremely warm.

Sexual Torture Room, museumgoers will find all sorts of perverse sexual devices, from spiked rape tools in which a male inserted his penis into a one-size-fits-all phallus that was then inserted into the woman, causing excruciating pain and death, to chastity belts for both men and women, to devious sawhorses designed to punish and torture women accused of heresy and witchcraft. These latter devices were also used as interrogation tools on men.

Folks in this area of the museum have reported hearing the sound of footsteps coming up and descending the ramp that leads to the Witches Torture Room. The sounds also come from the Guillotine Room. Even though guests can hear that someone is approaching on the ramp, no one can be seen. The ramp isn't the only part of these rooms where such phantom footfalls have been heard. They have also been heard in the Witches Room itself and in the Sexual Torture Room. Folks have also stated that there is something "wrong" in these rooms, especially the Witches Torture Room. Many people have said that while they are in this room they have felt as if they are not alone and that the feeling seems to come from the area where the masks are hanging. This same feeling comes over them in the Sexual Torture Room but nowhere near as strong as in the Witches Room.

The Witches Torture Room gives many guests the feeling of being watched, especially near the torture masks.

Not for the faint of heart, the Medieval Torture Museum shows man's inhumanity to man in ways that are almost impossible to believe were real.

A couple of other areas in the building have seen paranormal activity, and both are connected to the era when the building was a bank. In the Sexual Torture Room is a hidden bank vault that is now used as a storage space. Employees going into this vault to retrieve needed supplies have experienced the same type of activity as in the two adjacent museum rooms, but in a much more confined and intimate area. The other location is up on the first floor, where another bank vault is located. Not much happens here, but on a few occasions employees feel as if they are being watched from the shadows and that they are not alone.

The building housing the Medieval Torture Museum was built in the 1920s and has gone through many changes over the years. It is not known how many people passed away within its walls and how many of those may be haunting the place today. It is also likely haunted by spirit attachments belonging to some of the artifacts brought in to the museum from auctions and locations all over Europe. As I was waiting for Robert to escort me through the building, I spoke to an employee who had just been hired. He told me that on his first day of orientation, he was told that when closing up for the night he should "lock everything up as fast as you can and just leave, you don't want to be caught here for the ghosts to mess with you."

For the ParaTraveler, this is the sort of place they might want to add to their "must-see" list for this reason alone. For any tourist interested in the paranormal, please visit this unique museum. If for no other reason, the history alone is worth the visit. While there, try to remember our common humanity and say hello to those who may be stuck here due to inhumanity. Help them pass to a better rest beyond the veil.

15

EL COYOTE CAFÉ

The Great Depression was a hard time for the United States and the world. People lost all they had worked so hard to build and earn, including their jobs, homes and savings. Many people moved from the areas where they had grown up or left the only towns they had ever known to look for work and a better life among the ruins that America had become. Many people headed to California to look for work. George and Blanche March left Arizona for their neighboring state, not to find work but to create their own jobs and future by opening up what has become a staple in the community and a landmark in Hollywood.

When the Marches arrived in Los Angeles, they found a small site they could afford at the corner of First Street and La Brea Avenue between the cities of Los Angeles and Hollywood. This was where they opened their authentic Mexican café on March 5, 1931. The couple knew that even though the Depression was in full force, Hollywood was going strong and, as such, needed to eat and had the money to do so. George and Blanche were not only counting on the studio crowd to dine at their tiny little café but also hoping that by serving good food and ample portions for a reasonable price, average Angelinos would come as well. Their gamble paid off, and the Marches' Coyote Café began to make a name for itself and earned a steady customer base.

Because of the economic turmoil, the Marches were careful with their money, saved as much as they could in case the Depression became worse and began to build a nest egg for the future. When the Depression ended,

The roadside kitsch signage of the El Coyote Café seems out of place in today's Fairfax District.

it took a while for people to build back any semblance of wealth. But as the economy grew, so did the number of people coming to eat at El Coyote Café. It wasn't long before the Marches realized that if they wanted to keep growing and keep feeding the throngs of people coming to dine at their little café, they would have to find a bigger venue. It took some time, but the couple finally found the perfect location, in a predominantly Jewish neighborhood along busy Beverly Boulevard. So, in 1951, the Marches closed their original location and moved to the spot the restaurant still occupies today in the heart of the Fairfax District near Hollywood.

After moving into the new building, the Marches began to decorate the restaurant. They wanted to create a feeling of comfort and warmth so that when customers stepped inside, they felt welcome, as if they had just come home to family. The owners also wanted to give the café a feeling of authenticity, to bring folks not only the taste but also the feel of Mexico. The Marches created murals on the walls that depicted the art and culture of Mexico, hung vintage decor from south of the border and painted the entire café in the earthy colors for which Mexico is known. To add to the coziness of the restaurant, they installed dark red leather booths and glass-bottle windows. As part of the lighting, they strung warming Christmas lights throughout the café that hang all year. To make sure their restaurant would be noticeable to those passing by, they erected a large, red sign with bright yellow neon lights emblazoned with the words *El Coyote Mexican Food*. The sign is proudly displayed above the entrance. When the new café was opened, it had grown from a tiny eatery to an eight-room restaurant that could accommodate 375 guests, along with a stand-alone bar and patio dining.

Over the years, El Coyote Café has become something of a hot spot for Hollywood celebrities looking for good Mexican food. The bar and the foyer of the restaurant are now covered with autographed headshots

The El Coyote Café proudly displays photos left by world-famous and up-and-coming movie and TV stars.

of Hollywood stars dating from the early 1950s to modern times. Ricardo Montalbán, Grace Kelly and John Wayne were regulars. Today, the likes of Quentin Tarantino, Cuba Gooding Jr. and Seth Rogan can be found enjoying a tostada or enchilada and perhaps crispy tacos. The café has also become a movie star, having been featured in a couple of movies, television shows and photo shoots. Even with all of the good food, great atmosphere and star power at this wonderful café, it will always be marred by and associated with a tragic event on a fateful night in 1969, which the restaurant had nothing to do with and had no control over. During the incident, four lives were snuffed out by vicious killers.

On August 8, 1969, celebrity hairdresser Jay Sebring made reservations for dinner at the El Coyote Café for himself, ex-girlfriend Sharon Tate, Abigail Folger and her boyfriend, Wojciech Frykowski. Tate was more than eight months pregnant, and her husband, director Roman Polanski, had been out of the country for a while. Tate needed a bit of cheering up and some good company. The four friends decided to have a nice dinner at the café and then head back to Tate's home on Cielo Drive in Benedict Canyon and spend the rest of the evening enjoying one another's company. What happened after the group left the restaurant at 9:45 p.m. that night has become a horrific legend in the annals of brutality. All four friends would be savagely butchered by members of the Manson Family before the sun came up the next morning.

Even today, people flock to El Coyote Café to see the booth where Sharon Tate had her last meal of tamales and margaritas. Many wait a long time so they can be seated at the table, and some people order what Tate had. Tour companies bring their guests to the café—not to eat, but just to view the booth. Hollywood is home to many tour companies, including studio tours, tours of the stars' homes and even a few Hollywood "death tours." The latter will take you to the more, shall we say, dark tourist spots in and around Tinseltown. Many of these tour vans routinely stop at the restaurant and disgorge their guests, who wade into the restaurant, ignoring diners as they make their way to the "Tate Table." After a stop at El Coyote, guests on the death tours head up Benedict Canyon by way of Cielo Drive to see where Tate and her friends were killed. There was even a tour group that came into the restaurant every year on the anniversary of the killings to try to make contact with Tate, Sebring and the others.

There have been no sightings of Tate's or her friends' ghosts in the restaurant, and El Coyote says it would be odd if their spirits were there, as the victims weren't killed in the café. But that doesn't stop people from

The management and staff of El Coyote Café say that this table in a back corner of the restaurant is where Sharon Tate and her party ate the last meal of their lives.

believing the victims' ghosts are there, and it doesn't stop ghost hunters from coming to El Coyote in search of them, especially on the anniversary of the Manson murders. Just because Sharon Tate's and her friends' spirits aren't at the café, this doesn't mean that El Coyote isn't haunted. On the contrary, after I spoke with managers and employees at the restaurant, it seems there are a few ghosts here that can't get enough of the great food—or maybe it's the margaritas that keep them hanging around.

Bill, the general manager of the café, told me that many of the staff have had encounters with the resident spirits, and most believe they are harmless for the most part but that they can still be disturbing when unexpected. But many staff members would rather not have further contact with them. This is the main reason that many employees refuse to use the restroom in the back of the restaurant.

El Coyote Café is a large restaurant with three separate dining rooms and a dedicated bar area. The room in the back right of the café is also where banquets, special parties and events and other private functions are held. It is also where a haunted bathroom is located. The café's general manager, Bill, said he did not believe in ghosts until one evening when he was closing up and went into the back area to shut down the lights. He said that as

The restrooms in the back of the café are so haunted that many of the staff refuse to use them, instead using the main restrooms on the opposite side of the restaurant.

he went about flicking the light switches, the swinging door leading to the women's restroom began swinging erratically. He said that when he went to investigate why the door to the restroom was moving, he opened the door and saw someone or something there. The general manager thought, at that time, that it was a small boy he was seeing, and this was originally backed up by other employees who had seen this same spirit. But as more stories and sightings of this ghost have become known, it is now believed that the spirit is in fact Blanche March.

Blanche was not a tall or stout woman, and in life she would not have been mistaken for a boy. But then again, she also never tried to hide from her employees or guests and never tried to spy on them from darkened halls and doorways. It is possible that having a quick glimpse of the woman from the shadows might make one mistake her for a young boy. But the more this ghost is witnessed, the more obvious it becomes that it is likely Blanche keeping an eye on the café that she and her husband lovingly created. According to Marge Christoffersen, one of the owners of El Coyote Café and niece of George and Blanche March, "People have felt the spirit of my aunt. This place was her whole life. The atmosphere, the food, the customers." Keeping this in mind, it isn't hard to believe that she remains to this day.

It is possible that George March is still at the El Coyote as well. The general manager told me that above this same event room is the second floor of the restaurant. I was told that on many occasions, footsteps have been heard walking around both by guests and employees, even when it is known that no one is on the upper floor. It is standard practice for employees to double check this, as the café doesn't want to disturb their guests, and even though employees on occasion find another employee above, it is almost always empty of living souls. Many of the folks working at El Coyote Café believe that this spirit is George March and that he is still at the restaurant, either to help his wife keep an eye on things or because he is waiting for her so they can pass to the other side of the veil together. Of course, it could be a combination of both.

Another spirit who has become well known at the café is that of a woman named Margarita. She was a waitress at El Coyote and, according to the *Orange County Register*, may have also lived there at one time. According to café legend, Margarita was married to a violent, abusive man who, during one of his fits of rage, murdered the poor woman. Since the day Margarita was murdered, employees and guests of the restaurant have seen the beautiful woman inside the restaurant. One of the current waitresses at

Although the spirits of El Coyote Café can be found throughout the restaurant, it is the rear section that is said to be the most haunted.

the café has said that she thinks Margarita is a benevolent spirit and hopes that Margarita's evil, murdering husband isn't also hanging around the restaurant. So far, there is no indication that he is still there, nor is there any indication that any malicious ghost resides at El Coyote. On the contrary, all of the known ghosts seem to be quite polite, if not a bit shy.

The El Coyote Café has been open for more than ninety years and in that time has become an icon of the community and a gathering place for the local Jewish community. How many meals have been served to the gathering crowds will never be known. How many Hollywood stars both known and yet to be discovered have walked through the café's doors could be pondered from now until the end of time. One thing we do know beyond a shadow of a doubt is that the El Coyote Café has found a place not only in Hollywood legend and lore but also in history, because of one table and one meal on one fateful night in 1969. We the living will never forget that night, and many still stand vigil at the café on the anniversary of that event, as do the ghosts that call the El Coyote Café home in the afterlife.

16

THE SAD SPIRIT OF RAMON NOVARRO

Not many folks have heard of Ramon Novarro, and fewer still know about his brutal death at the hands of brothers who couldn't understand simple English phrases or the kindness of a gentle man who wanted nothing more than love and companionship. A gay man in Hollywood at a time when being gay was not tolerated, pressured by MGM to marry a woman he didn't love while being a silver-screen heartthrob, Novarro stayed true to himself and lived his life as he saw fit, not how others thought he should live. With all of the trials and tribulations related to his sexual preference and its unacceptance, as well as the pressures of Hollywood stardom and its decline as he grew older, Novarro never changed who he was or the kindness he showed to others, even when they may not have been kind to him.

Novarro was born José Ramón Samaniego in Durango, Mexico, in 1899. His father became concerned about the Mexican Revolution and how it might endanger his family. He figured that a move to the United States was the answer, and it didn't take long once they arrived for Ramon to adapt to his new country. When Ramon reached the age that he could get a job, he began working as a singing waiter while auditioning for roles in films. He was being cast only in bit parts, but he began to make connections in the industry, and two of them became friends: director Rex Ingram and his wife, Alice Terry. Knowing that Novarro had talent, they began promoting him as a rival to Rudolph Valentino. Knowing that audiences might have trouble pronouncing his real name, they suggested changing it to something easier.

Often compared with Rudolph Valentino, Ramon Novarro was a star in his own right.

Ramon was a close friend of Gabriel Navarro, the grandfather of rocker Dave Navarro, founder of the group Jane's Addiction. Ramon decided to use his friend's last name and his own middle name as his new stage persona. Unfortunately, due to a typing error, Ramon's new last name was spelled incorrectly, forever changing his name to Novarro.

Over the years, Novarro began to get bigger roles, and when Valentino took the young actor under his wing—and, some say, his bed—Novarro's star began to shine brighter. After Valentino's untimely death, Ramon Novarro took his place as Hollywood's heartthrob. Even though Novarro now knew that he was gay, he played his part toward the women of the world with dignity and aplomb. His studio, MGM, on the other hand, kept a close eye on Novarro to make sure he didn't ruin his and the studio's reputations. MGM even went so far as to order Novarro to marry a woman to keep suspicions about his sexuality as far from the minds of the public and the media as possible. Novarro refused.

Novarro was always discreet in his relationships and would meet his companions away from prying eyes. It is said that Novarro loved Valentino and that after the star died, Novarro found it hard to love another man. For a time, he found a bit of peace in the arms of his publicist, Herbert Howe, but it was always just for comfort and not for the love of the man. Novarro began drinking heavily and had bouts of depression, and this caused his performances to suffer. So, in 1935, his contract with MGM expired, and the studio failed to renew it. Over the next few years, Novarro struggled to find work. He began to take roles wherever he could find them, even taking a role in a Mexican-made drama. When television came on the scene, Novarro landed roles, mainly bit parts in a few Western films and took parts in TV shows such as *Walt Disney Presents*, *Dr. Kildare*, *Combat!*, *Bonanza* and *The Wild Wild West*.

By the late 1960s, Ramon Novarro had all but disappeared from public view, appearing only in the occasional TV show and on interview programs. One of these shows, *The Tonight Show*, would have a profound and deadly impact on his life. When Paul Ferguson saw Novarro on *The Tonight Show* and listened to Johnny Carson interview Ramon about having just finished remodeling his house, Ferguson was astonished when he heard Novarro admit that he had $5,000 in his new living room. Not intelligent enough to know that what Novarro was referring to was how much he had spent on the remodel, Ferguson made plans to steal the money he believed Ramon had hidden in his home. Ramon, who had grown tired of looking for men at bars and clubs around Hollywood, began to use an escort service to find the companionship he desired. The men at the service found Ramon to be a gentleman and one who didn't always require sex but just wanted company. They also knew him to pay well. One of these escorts knew Paul Ferguson and had given him Novarro's number so that Paul could connect with him as one of his companions.

Paul set up a meeting between himself, Ramon and Paul's brother Tommy to meet at Novarro's home so they could get to know one another. When the brothers arrived, Ramon met them at the door wearing a blue and red silk robe and offered them drinks. The men then relaxed before dinner. After dinner, Ramon invited Paul to his bedroom while brother Tommy talked on the phone to his girlfriend, who was in Chicago. Tommy was trying to keep his girlfriend from hearing the commotion that was going on in the other room, but when she said it sounded like someone was being killed, Tommy hung up and went to see what was going on. He walked in on Paul standing over Ramon, who was lying on the bed, bloody and bruised. Paul had beaten Ramon badly while trying to get him to reveal where the money was hidden in the living room. Ramon had no idea what Paul, and now his brother, were talking about, and he kept telling them that he had no money. The beating continued until Ramon was dead. The brothers fled with only the twenty dollars Ramon had in his robe.

When Ramon Novarro was found the next morning by his personal secretary, Edward Weber, his body had turned purple from the blood pooling in his muscles, and the bruises left by the Ferguson brothers were black. Ramon's eyes were swollen shut, and his lips were puffy and had turned blue. The autopsy stated: "Blood noted on the floor in bedroom, on ceiling and tooth noted lying on floor at foot of bed. Decedent's hands were tied behind his back with brown electric cord, (a white condom was found in decedent's right hand) and electric cord extended down and was tied around decedent's ankles. Lacerations and ecchymosis were noted on face and head." When the final autopsy report was released, it stated that Novarro's blood-alcohol level was .23, well above today's legal limit. He had a fractured nose with bruising on his head, chest, neck, left arm, knee and penis. The cause of death was determined to be "suffocation by choking on his own blood caused by multiple traumatic injuries of the face, neck, nose and mouth."

The Fergusons were caught, tried, found guilty of first-degree murder and sentenced to life in prison. They were both sent to San Quentin Prison in Northern California. The murder of a star as well known as Ramon Novarro was the type of case and trial to make the evening news across the country and around the world, and indeed it did, but for only a short time. Shortly after the death of Novarro, a series of murders took place that would shock the world and knock Ramon's death off the front pages. Charles Manson had struck.

Ramon may have been relegated to the third page of the newspapers and stricken from the evening news, but it seems that he was not ready to leave this mortal realm, and he remains to this day in the home that he built and loved. In the years since the murder took place, Novarro's house has been sold a number of times. Most of those who purchased the home stayed for only a short time and put the house back on the market. Many reasons were given for not staying, but most people understood the real reason for the people who came and went: Ramon's spirit was still in the home. The person who stayed the longest was the gentleman who bought the home specifically because Ramon haunted it. Unfortunately, he too lived there for a relatively short time before selling it to new buyers. For those who lived in the home and were brave enough to admit it was indeed haunted, the tales told were similar in nature. Novarro was often seen in the bedroom, and people claimed to watch as his spirit walked between the bed and the bathroom and then disappear near the shower. This sounds like a residual haunt in the wake of the traumatic death that Novarro endured at the hands of the Fergusons. Other visitors to the home have said they had "an uneasy" feeling

Ramon Novarro's death and trial would have received a lot more attention if not for Charles Manson and his "family's" killing spree.

inside. This happens mostly in the living room and dining room areas, where Novarro and his deadly guests spent time getting to know one another. This feeling may be of energy left by the Fergusons as they contemplated what they were about to do to this kindly old man, or it may be energy left behind by Ramon Novarro himself. Unfortunately, we may never know.

After the house was sold by the man wanting to live with Ramon's ghost, the new owners, a family, began to realize that the house was haunted. Not wanting to give up the choice property in Laurel Canyon, they decided that the best way to get rid of the ghost was to tear the house down and completely rebuild. As most people now know, that usually just makes things worse in terms of haunting activity. And that is exactly what happened. Once the house where Novarro had been murdered was demolished, the owners were sure that the hauntings would go away. But after the new house was built, the occurrences started back up. This time, as often happens, the hauntings actually increased. Neighbors and passersby report hearing screams and moans of pain, as well as the sound of a male voice asking someone or something to "please stop." Most people believe that these pleas are Novarro's spirit reliving his last horrific hours of life and begging the Fergusons to stop torturing him to death.

The house that replaced the home built by Novarro is said to have become even more haunted than its predecessor after the original home was torn down and replaced with the house in the photo.

In one amazing incident in the 1980s, news reporter Connie Chung, who was doing a news story about the life and death of Ramon Novarro, was filming at the house when several members of the film crew refused to enter. They said that as they were setting up in the house, an eerie feeling hit them and affected them so badly that they couldn't bring themselves to go past the threshold of the front door. One grip, who managed to go into the house before the rest of the crew, came running out, saying he had just seen Novarro in the bedroom. After he told the director he wouldn't go back inside, he promptly went home. Chung did manage to film the segment, but it took some effort to get it done, not to mention a lot more time than expected.

Not much has come from the house in many years related to paranormal activity, but one can imagine that Ramon is likely still there, enjoying the home he lived in and loved, even if it is not the same one he built. Maybe the family that lives there now has made peace with their resident spirit after finally realizing that Ramon is nothing more than a kind old man who wants acceptance and love. Let us hope he has found in death what he sought in life and that his afterlife is filled with the happiness he always missed.

17

THE ESCAPE HOTEL

A s we have seen, Hollywood is a town filled with change. Sometimes the changes are for good, sometimes the changes are for convenience and sometimes—and this is the norm—the changes are for the sake of change itself. There are, however, examples of Hollywood's past scattered around the city, spread out among its older sections and tucked in plain sight along many of its famous streets and byways. One of these old and historic buildings stands on Hollywood Boulevard, near many famous and infamous tourist locations and hot spots.

The building at 6633 Hollywood Boulevard began life between 1909 and 1911 as a drugstore with four tenement apartments on the second floor. The drugstore lasted for a few years, and when it shut its doors, the Jade Café took advantage of the great location and began serving customers from the space. The Jade Café lasted until the mid- to late 1930s. When a new owner bought the building, it was slated for demolition, and the café closed, much to the disappointment of its customers. There is some confusion about this period of the building's life. Some pictures show signs reading, "New owners, building coming down, new one to follow." One photo shows the Jade Café with a sign on its roof reading, "Owner will erect new building." One problem with these signs is that the building in the pictures looks remarkably like the same building we see today, with some modifications. It is more likely that sometime after these photos were taken, the new owner decided on a remodel instead of demolition and construction of a new structure.

No one is sure if the original building was torn down or remodeled, but what we do know is that the building that is now the Escape Hotel has gone through many iterations in its long life.

Whether the building was torn down or renovated is really a moot point. It has had a long and varied past. After Jade Café went out of business, Sontag Drugs opened on the site. It lasted for some time. Abe, Stern & Sons Furriers once occupied the property, and by the 1970s, Love's Wood Pit BBQ was serving ribs, chicken and beans. In the 1980s, the property went back to serving traditional diner food when the Hollywood Studio Café opened its doors. When that business failed, the space housed a nightclub, which lasted through the 1990s. There have been two possible murders in the building, one alleged to have taken place in the back hallway during the site's time as a nightclub. Regarding the other possible murder, Lee Hill-Chan, general manager of the Escape Hotel, told me about it during our interview. Lee said that a psychic once came into the lobby and said: "This place is haunted, isn't it? I know because I sense a family was murdered right by that window when the building was a café." The account told by the psychic can't be confirmed, nor can the murder of the nightclub patron, as Lee has been unable to locate any records.

When the current owners bought the property, they began renovating it into the wonderful Escape Hotel. With several escape room challenges set among the art deco and creepy atmosphere of a 1930s hotel, à la Disney's Tower of Terror, visitors find themselves drawn into the past, and this makes the game both more real and more frightening than most other escape rooms. For those hooked on escape room challenges, the ghostly ambiance of the venue is one that can't be passed up. When the gamers find out that the Escape Hotel is inhabited by real spirits, it makes the teams more determined to complete the game before the spirits decide to lend a haunting—I mean helping—hand.

During my interview with general manager Lee Hill-Chan, he told me that he believes there are "hot spots" of paranormal activity in the building and that one of them is right off of the lobby of the "hotel" itself. The area in question is where the photo booth and the hallway leading to various escape rooms and the restrooms are located. On the wall opposite the photo booth is a table that had several juggling pins on top of it. One night, while Lee was working, he heard a loud crash come from the area. When he went to investigate, he found that one of the pins was lying on the floor, several feet from the table where it belonged. There was no one else nearby, and if the pin had simply fallen off its perch, it would be on the floor next to the table. Lee checked the security cameras a little while later and discovered that they had caught the pin flying from the table but not the moment of impact. It was as if the pin had flown or been thrown from the table in order to land so far away. So far, no one has been able to replicate the pin moving that far from its original location, and no one has been able to determine how it actually moved from the table.

Another strange occurrence in this hot spot in the hallway took place when Lee was walking down the hall from the back toward the lobby area and received a radio call from a coworker, who was watching the security monitors. The man wanted to know who the woman following Lee was. Lee, a bit confused, looked around, saw no one and asked his fellow employee what he was talking about. When Lee finally got back to the control room, his associate told him that a woman had been following Lee. Lee, just as adamantly, told the employee that there hadn't been anyone else in the hallway.

One morning while Lee rounded the corner by the staircase, he noticed a wide-open door at the end of the hallway. This was the door closest to the table with the juggling pins. As the room was in the process of being renovated into a new escape room, Lee figured the design/construction coordinator was busy at work and getting an early start. As he walked down the hallway, the door slowly closed and latched as if someone had shut it.

The 1930s style, mixed with Halloween kitsch and an atmosphere of luxury in the lobby, lets one know from the moment they enter the Escape Hotel that they are in for an interesting and fun time.

When Lee got to the end of the hall, he stopped, opened the door and started to call out "good morning" to the design coordinator, Frank. That is when he noticed that the room was empty of all living beings. Neither Frank nor anyone else was in the room.

One more thing of note happened in this area. It was on a Monday evening, and Lee was training a new hire. The Escape Hotel is closed on Mondays, so it is a perfect day to conduct training sessions, as there are no guests to disturb. Lee told me that as he and the trainee were standing by the photo booth, they heard a loud bang come from the Haunted Fair game room. There was no one else in the building, they found no one in the game room and they found nothing amiss. This room just happens to be right across from the room where Lee thought Frank had closed the door.

One of the cast members of the Escape Hotel told me about a strange incident that took place in the Day Care room. One of the props used in the game is a doll. After the team that had been in this escape room finished, the cast member went into the Day Care room to reset all of the clues and props for the next team. All but one of the props could be found; the doll, a main clue item, was nowhere to be seen. After looking a second time, the cast member brought in a fresh pair of eyes to help look, but the doll was still not found. After checking the monitors, they found that no one had taken the prop. It had simply disappeared. A little while later, they went back to the escape room, and there, sitting in the middle of the floor, was the doll, in the center of the room, upright and staring at them. Reviewing the monitors to see if someone had put the doll back, they found that the time stamp on the camera froze for a brief second, and immediately on unfreezing, the doll was sitting on the floor. There was no time during which someone could have put the prop back in the room.

This was not the only time when the monitors have "glitched" at the same time strange things happened. One night, when Lee Hill-Chan was resetting the Attic game room and wearing the standard headphones, he began to hear a girl's voice come over the headset. It was a bit distorted, to the point that Lee was unable to make out the words. But the tenor of the voice was "kinda panicked." Lee was afraid it might be April, the girl working the front lobby, so he called down to make sure she was OK. Later, when he looked at the monitors, he saw a strange misty figure appear behind him and take the shape of a woman, seemingly wearing a dress or a cloak from an earlier period in Hollywood history. The strange thing about this manifestation is that at the same time the possible apparition was seen, the time stamp on the camera jumped ahead two minutes, stayed there for just a second and then jumped back to the actual time. This may seem like a simple glitch, but once the camera jumped back, there was no sign of Lee in the video clip, even though he was still in the room and in the same spot he had been in before the camera jumped ahead. Lee also said that he noticed that the flashlight he was carrying that night constantly flickered while he was in the Attic but worked fine outside the room. Since that day, his flashlight has worked fine in the Attic room.

This hallway seems to have its fair share of paranormal activity, from doors opening on their own to objects being tossed from shelves.

A little while after the Attic room reset, Lee was back upstairs, assisting a team, when each member heard loud knocking as they were walking down the hall. The team members said they had heard the same knock coming from the game room next to theirs, lasting throughout their entire game session. They said it sounded as if someone was trying to get the attention of someone else or perhaps asking to be let out of the other room. Lee was surprised to hear that there was knocking coming from that particular room, and the team was surprised to find out that the room was empty now and had been empty the entire time they played their game. One further report from this area comes from a cast member named Lilli, who said that while she was in the Attic room she could smell something "bad" coming from the room, a smell of rotten eggs or sulfur.

April had her own experience one morning as she came in to open the facility. She had taken care of the downstairs area, but as she headed up to the lounge and bar area, she could hear someone snoring loudly. She thought someone might have broken in to sleep and get out of the elements. She decided to leave and went outside to wait for her coworker to arrive. When the two of them went back inside, the snoring had stopped and there was no one inside and no sign of a break-in. During my interview with Lee, a new hire sat with us and mentioned that both she and Lee had heard snoring that morning in the same area where April heard the same noise.

Ivan, the owner of the Escape Hotel, told me that he had a certain pen he liked to use, one that was special to him. One day while working, he discovered that the pen was missing. He said he had searched his desk and his entire office and still couldn't find it. He asked a friend and coworker if he had borrowed the pen. His friend said he had not. While the two of them looked around the office, another coworker entered and asked what they were doing. When Ivan stopped to answer, all three heard something fall from the ceiling onto the desk. What fell from on high was Ivan's favorite pen.

King, one of the cast members, told me about a time when he and a few other game masters who were watching the game monitors heard the power saw in the workshop of design/construction coordinator Frank turn on. A couple of them thought that Frank had already gone home for the night, but looking at the cameras, they could see that Frank was still in the building, but in another room far from his workspace. Two of the people in the group headed over to the workshop. The others refused to go, saying that it sounded as if someone was cutting wood. As the two employees neared the workshop door, the saw suddenly shut off. When they entered the room, there was no sign that anyone was there, and when they checked the saw, they found that it had a safety switch that had to be held down by a human hand for the saw to operate. The only way in or out was the door they had come through, and they had heard the saw shut off moments before they opened the door.

The bar directly above the haunted hallway has its own tales of haunting activity. Keep an eye out for spirits while you enjoy sipping on your spirits.

One morning before Lee became general manager, as he was opening the hotel and turning on lights, he was upstairs behind the bar and walking back to the lounge when he saw one of his coworkers through the window behind the bar. He thought to himself, "Oh, cool, he is helping turn on the lights." About ten minutes later, Lee was back downstairs behind the front desk when this coworker came in, apologizing for being late. Lee looked at him and asked the man if he had been there, left and come back. But the man told him that he had been running late and had just arrived. To this day, Lee has no idea who or what he saw that morning.

There is a game room in the basement called the Cursed Crypt, and it proved so popular that the owners decided to add a second escape room based on this one, to be called Black Forest. One day, Lee decided to go down and have a look at the progress of the creation but found that as he walked into the space, a wave of dread washed over him. He said that he could feel something telling him to "Get the fu** out." Lee said he ran from the room and was afraid to look behind him out of fear of what he might find and he also slightly twisted his ankle in his haste. Lee said that was the only time he ever felt afraid or threatened in the building and that it has not happened since.

The basement seems to be another hot spot at the Escape Hotel. One of the most interesting paranormal occurrences took place in the Cursed Crypt. One evening while Lee was resetting the Cursed Crypt, Lilli, a coworker, was watching the cameras and reported to Lee that she was seeing a shadow walking around in the office room of that particular game. After she reported this, one of two "fuses," props for the game, flew out of its fuse box and landed about five feet from its box. These props are not light. They are made of metal, so they don't bounce. In the video, the prop flies from its perch, and what looks like a little girl's head peeks from behind the doorjamb of the office room, almost as if she was the one who tossed the fuse prop. Lee and others have tried to recreate the prop falling and landing as far away as it did, but so far none of these attempts have come close to replicating the event.

In this room, a paranormal team investigating the Escape Hotel was using a spirit box, which repeatedly said "Steven." This is the name of Lee's

This is where Lee, the general manager of the Escape Hotel, saw a prop fly from its perch just before he watched the head of a little ghost girl peek around the corner.

husband. The spirit box also repeated the word "sleep." Steven wasn't at the hotel that night but was in fact at home sleeping. It's possible that the spirits were trying to tell Lee that they knew about Steve and liked them both. Or perhaps the spirits were recommending that Lee go home to join his husband in slumber. The team also heard knocking coming from the room behind the Office room. The odd thing about this is that the room the knocking came from is actually a storage closet, and no one was anywhere near it during the investigation.

The appearance of the little girl on camera isn't surprising when one takes into account that Lee, who has done some incredible research into the history of the building, believes that, at a minimum, the Escape Hotel is haunted by a little girl and her mother. Frank has said that in the seven years he has been there, he has seen the little girl five or six times playing on most of the stairways. The snoring that is heard in the upstairs lounge could be coming from someone who lived in one of the tenement apartments in the earlier days of the building. Maybe someday we will find out who these souls are.

Whether you are a history buff, a Hollywood fan or an escape room artist, the Escape Hotel on Hollywood Boulevard is a must-see attraction. It offers creepy decor and beautiful ambiance, and just walking into the place fills visitors with nostalgia and a feeling of adventure. If only for the spirits of the past, the Escape Hotel is a place the intrepid ParaTraveler should consider putting on their bucket list. Just remember: if you get stuck in one of the games and can't seem to figure out how to escape, all you need to do is ask one of the resident spirits for help. After all, they know the ins and outs of the rooms. Of course, asking them for help might also be considered cheating.

18

THE MANSION

Laurel Canyon, in the Hollywood Hills, was once where Tinseltown's actors and actresses bought homes and held court for friends, relatives and, on occasion, fans. Clara Bow, Tom Mix and Bessie Love all called the canyon home in the early days of Hollywood. During the "talkie" era, Ramon Novarro, Lew Ayres and Wallace Reid took up residence among the trees of the Hollywood Hills. After rock 'n' roll came on the scene, Laurel Canyon became the place to be, with people like Frank Zappa, Graham Nash and Jim Morrison moving in for the peace and quiet the area provided and as a conducive setting for them to create their music. And, of course, to party. Laurel Canyon also saw its fair share of grisly murders. Ramon Novarro was killed by two brothers who didn't fully understand the English language, and the Wonderland Murders shocked the country with their brutality and connection to perhaps the most famous porn star in history. Laurel Canyon has seen it all, including a mystery surrounding the greatest magician who ever lived. And there is the story of two mansions, one of which is caught up in a mystery in which it was never directly involved.

Once the home of Errol Flynn, the house on Laurel Canyon Boulevard now known simply as the Mansion was built in 1918. (There is some speculation that it was erected in 1925.) The home was built on one and three-quarters acres of prime land in the canyon. After Flynn moved out of the Mansion, it went through a series of owners and famous renters. It is said that at one time or another W.C. Fields lived in the home, it became a home for "wayward women" and Benjamin "Bugsy" Siegel occupied it. During the devastating Laurel Canyon fire of 1959, the mansion and thirty-seven other homes were destroyed. The mansion's lot sat vacant for some time.

The house was rebuilt as a ten-bedroom villa. Jimi Hendrix briefly lived in the home, and Mick Jagger and David Bowie were long-term guests. The home went through several owners until record producer and former co-president of Columbia Records Rick Rubin purchased the estate as his home and eventually began using it as a recording studio. Rubin didn't initially use the property for recording, but after the Red Hot Chili Peppers used the estate to make their album *Blood Sugar Sex Magik* in 1991, and it went smoothly, Rubin decided it was the perfect place to record music and film videos. That same year, Guns N' Roses recorded their song "November Rain" at what was now being called simply the Mansion.

Starting in 1999, the Mansion served as a studio for many groups and solo artists, including Slipknot, System of a Down, Linkin Park, Maroon 5, Jay-Z and Marilyn Manson. The group that started it all, the Red Hot Chili Peppers, recorded at the Mansion three more times, for the songs "Fortune Faded" and "Save the Population" and the albums *Greatest Hits* and *Stadium Arcadium*. It was during this time that rumors of the Mansion being haunted came to light.

It is not clear how the confusion came to be, but somehow folks began to confuse the Mansion with the Houdini Estate just down the hill from the recording studio. Maybe it has to do with the fact that both estates have a reputation for hauntings, or maybe it is because many people believe the Houdini Estate is called the Houdini Mansion and confuse references to the Mansion with that of the misnamed Houdini Estate. In any case, so many websites get these names wrong that it is no wonder the confusion between the two exists. One well-known and widely read website that I myself use for research tells the story of the Mansion while calling it the Houdini Mansion. It mixes the stories of these two estates so seamlessly that if this is the only site someone looks to for information on the Mansion, they will think the two estates are one and the same. From tales of Harry Houdini walking the grounds of the Houdini Estate to him wandering the hallways and rooms of the Mansion, the mistaken spirits of the two homes may now be as confused as the living.

Regardless of the mixing of the two tales, the Mansion seems to be more haunted than the Houdini Estate is or ever has been. It's been said that the Mansion became haunted almost from the time the home was built in the early twentieth century. There is an unverified story that one night while hosting a party in his new home, the wealthy owner's son got into an argument with his lover. Things escalated, and the son threw his lover over the balcony railing to his death. The father, not wanting to see his son go to jail, spent his fortune defending the boy. People say that from that moment on, the house became not only haunted but also cursed. Many people over the years have claimed to see the spirit of a young man, dressed in clothes from the 1920s, on one of the balconies. Those who see him wonder who he might be and are surprised when he simply fades from view without having ever moved. Could this be the son's lover, unable to move on after the man he loved killed him in cold blood?

As at the Houdini Estate, there are said to be tunnels under the Mansion. These tunnels are believed to lead to what was once an illicit liquor store near the estate. Supposedly, these tunnels were used during Prohibition to smuggle liquor to the house. The tunnel supposedly found in the basement of the Mansion was said to be fifteen to twenty feet high and extended straight into the mountain in the direction of the bootleg liquor store. The tunnel has since been closed off for safety reasons, but it might be why folks at the estate see spirits dressed in fancy clothes waiting by the now-covered tunnel.

Rick Rubin's publicist, Heidi Robinson-Fitzgerald, once had an encounter in the house that she says she can never forget. She said in an interview that it "was freaky" and that she can still remember how it made her feel. Heidi went on to say that when System of a Down was recording at the Mansion, she was organizing interviews and photoshoots one morning before anyone else had arrived at the house. She said she was sitting in the dining room facing the grand staircase with her back to the entryway. Suddenly, she felt something behind her. "It wasn't bad or anything but it was obvious and it grew to where it was so intense that I felt like something was standing right behind me." Heidi went on to say that she looked behind her but nothing was there, until she turned back around. When she looked back to the stairs, she said a woman appeared in front of her on the stairs, dressed all in white and walking down the steps. "There was no breeze in the house but whatever she was wearing was fluttering in the wind." The woman stopped, but Heidi couldn't tell if the ghost saw her or not. Then the spirit turned around, walked back up the stairs and vanished.

Many of the bands recording and staying at the Mansion have had experiences with the ghosts of the estate. While living at the Mansion during the recording of their album *Vol. 3: (The Subliminal Verses)*, Slipknot reported a few odd occurrences. Lead singer Corey Taylor snapped a picture of two strange lights hovering near the thermostat. He said these lights changed the temperature in his room. According to what Corey wrote in his book

The Mansion is near the very haunted Hollywood Boulevard. Could some of the spirits at the Mansion have come from Hollywood to enjoy the luxurious accommodations the home has to offer?

A Funny Thing Happened on the Way to Heaven (Da Capo Press, 2014), he also saw a full-body apparition, but not the same lady in white seen by Rubin's publicist. According to Taylor, he was taking a shower in his locked room when he heard something just outside the bathroom. Soaking wet and with soap in his eyes, he looked up and saw the ghost of a man walking across his room. The spirit was attired in a full tuxedo with tails. Needless to say, Taylor quickly rinsed, got dressed and left the room. Drummer Joey Jordison claimed that every morning while staying at the house, the door to his room opened by itself precisely at 4:00 a.m.

System of a Down guitarist Daron Malakian said that every day at the same time all of his amps began to act strange. Unlike Jordison, whose bedroom door opened at 4:00 a.m., Malakian's amps would go wonky at 4:00 p.m. The Mars Volta, a lesser-known band that was staying at the Mansion in 2003, reported seeing several doors opening on their own throughout the house, not unlike what Jordison experienced. But in the band's case, moving doors weren't limited to those in bedrooms. Other bands and crew have reported seeing doors opening and closing with no one there to move the doors.

The Red Hot Chili Peppers, the band that has recorded at the Mansion more than any other, had its own strange happenings there. Guitarist John

Frusciante swears he heard the sound of a woman engaged in sexual activity and that it sounded as if she was really enjoying herself. This event, coupled with the belief that they caught a spirit on camera, caused drummer Chad Smith to refuse to stay at the house. Even though Smith believed that the spirits were probably not dangerous, he thought it best to stay clear of them. Frusciante considered the ghosts friendly. I suppose that, knowing the spirits don't mind a bit of voyeurism, Frusciante's belief might be justified.

It is a shame that the Houdini Estate and the Mansion have now become so confused that many people no longer believe they are two different locations. Both have long histories, both have seen celebrities living and performing there and both have plenty of ghost stories. As we have seen with the stories from both locations, the amount of activity at the Mansion far outweighs what takes place at the Houdini Estate. That said, it is truly sad if we don't realize their individuality and the different ghosts that reside at each. The Mansion is only a short distance from the Houdini Estate, so it makes one wonder if the spirits are aware of their seeming lack of individuality and could be upset that folks have done this to them.

EPILOGUE

Some people think Hollywood is a magical place where all you have to do is sit down in a diner and be discovered by a movie producer or a talent agent. Others believe that working in a restaurant in Hollywood will eventually allow them to meet and impress those same movie moguls, who in turn will make them a star and a millionaire. As we have seen, these dreams of stardom, even in the rare instances in which they do come true, can come at a steep price, possibly even the cost of one's life. So, the next time you are sitting comfortably on your couch, watching your favorite television show or old movie, or munching popcorn in the movie theater, take a moment to think about the actors and actresses on the screen. Who are they? Who were they? What are their real lives like? And, if dead, how did they die and how did they live?

To most people, the movies are a diversion, an escape from reality for a short time and a way to unwind after a long day at work. Many people don't stop to think that those on the screen and behind it are people, just like us, with their own lives and dreams for the future, working to give the public the pleasure of the diversions they create. As people themselves, they have the same problems and stresses we all do, and probably many other problems we will never understand. Stardom has its drawbacks, including fans never leaving their idols alone when the stars are simply trying to have a quiet meal out and people with maps constantly driving by the stars' homes. Privacy is a thing of the past. Keep all of this in mind the next time you watch a TV show or movie. As we have seen in these pages, many Hollywood figures may still be on this side of the veil. They may have unfinished business or are trying to help others avoid the same mistakes, pitfalls and deaths they had to endure.

Bibliography

Books

Clune, Brian. *Hollywood Obscura*. Atglen, PA: Schiffer Books, 2017.

Jacobson, Laurie, and Marc Wanamaker. *Hollywood Haunted*. Rev. ed. Santa Monica, CA: Angel City Press, 1999.

Ogden, Tom. *Haunted Hollywood*. 2nd ed. Essex, CT: Globe Pequot, 2015.

Websites

Chapter 1

Degrushe, Allison. "Will the Best Actress Curse Prevail at the 95th Academy Awards? We Hope Not!" Distractify, March 9, 2022. https://www.distractify.com.

Meccleston. "The Curse of the Best Actress Oscar." Best for Film, May 10, 2011. https://bestforfilm.com.

Mirror. "Oscars' Best Actress Curse? Everyone from Sandra Bullock to Kate Winslet Have Suffered Heartbreak Following Win." February 28, 2016. www.mirror.co.uk.

Soares, Andre. "Luise Rainer: Oldest Living Academy Award Winner + the 'Oscar Curse.'" Alt Film Guide. https://altfg.com.

Chapter 2

American Hauntings. "Was 'The Exorcist' Cursed?" https://www.americanhauntingsink.com.

Felthousen-Post, Cyn. "The Curse of The Exorcist: Behind the Scenes of the Scariest Movie Ever Made." Groovy History, October 12, 2019. https://groovyhistory.com.

Chapter 3

Moreno, Abeni. "Was 'The Crow' Cursed? Inside the Tragic Death of Brandon Lee." Film Daily, October 26, 2021. https://filmdaily.co.

Real Unexplained Mysteries. "The Bruce Lee Family Curse." https://realunexplainedmysteries.com.

Shelton, Jacob. "'The Crow' May Have Been Cursed—And Not Just Because of Brandon Lee's Death." Ranker, July 29, 2020. https://www.ranker.com.

Chapter 4

Jackson, Matthew. "13 Devilish Facts about *Rosemary's Baby*." Mental Floss, October 4, 2017. https://www.mentalfloss.com.

Shelton, Jacob. "All the Spooky Evidence That *Rosemary's Baby* Might Be a Cursed Movie." Ranker, March 26, 2021. https://www.ranker.com.

Chapter 5

Dimuro, Gina. "How Did James Dean Die? Inside the Accident That Killed the Beloved Actor." All That's Interesting, February 13, 2022. https://allthatsinteresting.com.

Eyes on Cinema. "Alec Guinness Warned James Dean One Week Before His Death." YouTube, May 20, 2015. www.youtube.com.

Pic Tell Me. "How James Dean Predicted His Death." https://www.pictellme.com.

Chapter 6

Homer, Aaron, and Amy Beeman. "How Oliver Reed Predicted His Own Death." Grunge, October 21, 2021. https://www.grunge.com.

Chapter 7

Fiorentino, Alyssa. "How the Former Home of Actress Jean Harlow Became One of Hollywood's Darkest Mysteries." *House Beautiful*, October 13, 2021. https://www.housebeautiful.com.

House and History. "Jay Sebring House: A House Packed with History!" https://houseandhistory.com.

Veliz, Leslie. "Why Some Aren't Convinced Jean Harlow's Husband Paul Bern Died by Suicide." Grunge, August 30, 2022. https://www.grunge.com.

Chapter 8

Agius, Nicola. "Carrie Fisher 'Predicted Date of Her Own Death by Writing It on Head of Princess Leia Cutout'." Mirror, February 19, 2017. https://www.mirror.co.uk.
Chavez, Nicole, and Steve Almasy. "Coroner Releases Findings in Carrie Fisher's Death." CNN, June 17, 2017. https://www.cnn.com.

Chapter 9

Huliq, James. "John Lennon's Psychic Predicted His Death, While '9' Significant for the Beatle." Huliq, November 7, 2011. https://huliq.com.
Southerland, Jude. "Number 9, Number 9 (and John Lennon)." Culture Sonar, February 12, 2022. https://www.culturesonar.com.

Chapter 10

Bradford, Chris. "Tupac Mystery: Tupac Chillingly 'Predicted' Exact Age of His Own Death and Said 'I Know How I'll Die' Before Killing, Claims Pal." Sun, April 14, 2022. https://www.thesun.co.uk.
Forrester, Katy. "Did Prince Predict His Own Death?" Mirror, April 21, 2016. https://www.mirror.co.uk.
Heintz, Megan. "'Glee' Actress Naya Rivera Posted About Death Days Before Going Missing: 'Tomorrow Is Not Promised'." *In Touch Weekly*, July 9, 2020. https://www.intouchweekly.com.
Heller, Corinne. "Prince Predicted His Own Death, Sister Says." E News, March 15, 2017. https://www.eonline.com.
Mendoza, Jean. "This Is How Tupac Predicted His Own Death." Grunge, July 22, 2021. https://www.grunge.com.
Varghese, Johnlee. "Naya Rivera Dead: Glee Star Predicted Her Death through Eminem's Song About Drowning, Fan Theory." International Business Times, July 11, 2020. https://www.ibtimes.sg.

Chapter 11

King, Susan. "Restless Spirits." *Los Angeles Times*, October 31, 2011. https://www.latimes.com.
Meares, Hadley. "Prisoners of Fame: Falcon Lair, Rudolph Valentino, Doris Duke, and the Cult of Celebrity Death." KCET, January 14, 2016. https://www.kcet.org.

Chapter 13

Britannica. "Harry Houdini." April 28, 2023. https://www.britannica.com.

Houdini's Ghost. "Houdini Is Haunting the Right Garden." http://www. houdinisghost.com. Photos of Houdini at the pool.

———. "Houdini Lived at 2435 Laurel Canyon Blvd. But He Swam at 2400 Laurel Canyon Blvd." http://www.houdinisghost.com. Photo of Christmas party.

Wild About Harry. "The True Story of the Laurel Canyon Houdini Estate." March 30, 2012. https://www.wildabouthoudini.com.

Chapter 15

Carter, Noelle. "64 Bottles of Tequila, Halloween Costumes and Maybe a Ghost at El Coyote." *Lost Angeles Times*, October 28, 2016. https://www.latimes.com.

Orange County (CA) Register. "Been There Forever: El Coyote in LA Evokes Classic Kitsch." November 19, 2014. https://www.ocregister.com.

Chapter 18

Laurel Canyon Guitars Online. "Laurel Canyon History." http:// laurelcanyonguitarsonline.com.

Vrchoticky, Nicholas. "The Spooky Truth About the Mansion Recording Studio." Grunge, December 8, 2020. https://www.grunge.com.

ABOUT THE AUTHOR

Brian Clune is the cofounder and historian for Planet Paranormal Radio and Planet Paranormal Investigations. He has traveled the entire state of California, researching its haunted hot spots and historical locations in an effort to bring knowledge of the paranormal and the wonderful history of the state to those interested in learning about them.

His interest in history has led him to volunteer aboard the USS *Iowa* and at the Fort MacArthur Military Museum, and he has given lectures at colleges and universities around the state. He has been involved with numerous TV shows, including *Ghost Adventures*, *My Ghost Story*, *Dead Files* and *Ghost Hunters*, and was the subject in a companion documentary for the movie *Paranormal Asylum*. He has also appeared on numerous local, national and international radio programs. Clune is the cohost of the radio program *The Full Spectrum Project*, which deals in subjects such as ghosts, murders and all things odd and weird—both natural and supernatural.

His other books include *California's Historic Haunts* (Schiffer Books) and the highly acclaimed *Ghosts of the Queen Mary* (The History Press), as well as *Ghosts and Legends of Alcatraz* (The History Press) and *Ghosts and Legends of Calico* (The History Press), all with coauthor Bob Davis. Brian and Bob also teamed up to write the riveting biography of Ghost Box creator Frank Sumption. Clune is also the author of *Haunted San Pedro* (The History

Press) and *Hollywood Obscura* (Schiffer Books), the latter a spellbinding book dealing with Hollywood's dark and sordid tales of murder and ghosts. Clune is currently working on other titles for The History Press and is teaching courses in paranormal studies at California State University–Dominguez Hills.

Clune lives in Southern California with his loving wife, Terri, his three wonderful children and, of course, Wandering Wyatt!

OTHER BOOKS BY BRIAN CLUNE

Ghosts of the Queen Mary (The History Press, 2014)
California's Historic Haunts (Schiffer Books, 2015)
Haunted San Pedro (History Press, 2016)
Hollywood Obscura: Death, Murder and the Paranormal Aftermath
(Schiffer Books, 2017)
Haunted Universal Studios (The History Press, 2018)
Ghosts and Legends of Alcatraz (The History Press, 2019)
Thinking outside the Box: Frank Sumption, Creator of the Ghost Box
(Palmetto Publishing, 2019)
Ghosts and Legends of Calico (The History Press, 2020)
Haunted Heart of San Diego (The History Press, 2021)
Legends and Lore Along California's Highway 395 (The History Press, 2022)
California's Haunted Route 66 (The History Press, 2022)
Haunted Southern California (The History Press, 2022
Dark Tourism: California (Schiffer Books, 2022)

Brian Clune and his book *Ghosts of the Queen Mary* were featured in *LIFE
Magazine: World's Most Haunted Places: Creepy, Ghostly and Notorious Spots*
(LIFE, 2016)

FREE eBOOK OFFER

Scan the QR code below, enter your e-mail address and get our original Haunted America compilation eBook delivered straight to your inbox for free.

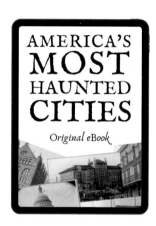

ABOUT THE BOOK

Every city, town, parish, community and school has their own paranormal history. Whether they are spirits caught in the Bardo, ancestors checking on their descendants, restless souls sending a message or simply spectral troublemakers, ghosts have been part of the human tradition from the beginning of time.

In this book, we feature a collection of stories from five of America's most haunted cities: Baltimore, Chicago, Galveston, New Orleans and Washington, D.C.

SCAN TO GET
AMERICA'S MOST HAUNTED CITIES

Having trouble scanning? Go to:
biz.arcadiapublishing.com/americas-most-haunted-cities